FIRST
SOLDIERS
DOWN

FIRST SOLDIERS DOWN

CANADA'S FRIENDLY FIRE DEATHS IN AFGHANISTAN

RON CORBETT

DUNDURN
TORONTO

Project Editor: Michael Carroll
Editor: Cheryl Hawley
Design: Jesse Hooper
Printer: Webcom

Library and Archives Canada Cataloguing in Publication

Corbett, Ron, 1959-
    First soldiers down : Canada's friendly fire deaths in Afghanistan / Ron Corbett ; foreword by Pat Stogran.

Issued also in electronic formats.
ISBN 978-1-4597-0327-8

    1. Friendly fire (Military science)--Afghanistan. 2. Afghan War, 2001- --Aerial operations, American. 3. Canada--Armed Forces--Afghanistan. 4. Canada. Canadian Armed Forces. Princess Patricia's Canadian Light Infantry. 5. Canada--Military relations--United States. 6. United States--Military relations--Canada. I. Title.

DS371.4.C57 2012   958.104'7   C2011-908029-X

1 2 3 4 5   16 15 14 13 12

We acknowledge the support of the **Canada Council for the Arts** and the **Ontario Arts Council** for our publishing program. We also acknowledge the financial support of the **Government of Canada** through the **Canada Book Fund** and **Livres Canada Books**, and the **Government of Ontario** through the **Ontario Book Publishing Tax Credit** and the **Ontario Media Development Corporation**.

Care has been taken to trace the ownership of copyright material used in this book. The author and the publisher welcome any information enabling them to rectify any references or credits in subsequent editions.

J. Kirk Howard, President

Printed and bound in Canada.
www.dundurn.com

Dundurn
3 Church Street, Suite 500
Toronto, Ontario, Canada
M5E 1M2

Gazelle Book Services Limited
White Cross Mills
High Town, Lancaster, England
LA1 4XS

Dundurn
2250 Military Road
Tonawanda, NY
U.S.A. 14150

Dedicated to the 3rd Battalion,
Princess Patricia's Canadian Light Infantry Battle Group, 2002

CONTENTS

FOREWORD

It is my privilege to have played a part in the now-historical Operation APOLLO. I think APOLLO was a landmark mission for Canada and it is a testament to the legacy of service and professionalism in the Canadian Forces, built by our veterans and being perpetuated by those who continue to answer the call and make the sacrifices for our country. I also feel that the so-called "friendly fire" incident is a very important event in our ever-evolving military history.

Op APOLLO was Canada's first military engagement in a new security environment — similar to the new security environment precipitated by the former-Soviet Union that resulted in the formation of NATO in 1949. Unlike the industrial-style warfare that characterized the Cold War, Op APOLLO was the threshold of an era of information-age warfare. International terrorists and transnational criminals now pose serious threats to all legitimate nation states. With access to huge sums of money from narcotic trade, they now have access to technology for weapons of mass destruction, broadband global communications, high-speed world-wide travel, and satellite imagery — capabilities that used to be the sole domain of national military organizations.

Sometimes described as a global insurgency, terrorists are capable of hijacking entire countries, such as Afghanistan, and inflicting monstrous destruction and havoc, like they did on 9-11. To the innocent civilians whom they hide among, their actions are portrayed as a popular, albeit perverted, war of ideals. This type of warfare has displaced the industrial-style mass destruction that emerged from the world wars of the twentieth century.

This war is being waged as much in the minds of everybody as it is on the battlefield; our tolerance for casualties and collateral damage is virtually non-existent. We know and will always remember the first Canadians who were killed in action: Sergeant Marc Léger, Corporal Ainsworth Dyer, and Privates Nathan Smith and Richard Green.

I've helped others who have written about the friendly fire incident, but I am always willing to engage. I have come to believe that nobody's personal perspective ever reflects ground truth, not even my own. Many times I have unabashedly thrown down the gauntlet of my take on issues and events, not so much to draw a line in the sand, but more as an invitation to others to shape my perception on reality. That's why I initially agreed to help Ron with his project.

Since I agreed to work with him, I told Ron virtually everything I could remember about the historic "rendezvous with destiny" of the Apollo-Rakkasans and the notorious friendly fire incident — from my point of view — and handed over all of the notes and clippings that I held onto for posterity. To round out his appreciation of the incident I introduced him to as many of the people from the Apollo-Rakkasan Battle Group as I could, encouraging them all to contribute their unabashed recollections and opinions — the good the bad and the ugly — so that history would have a broad and uncensored record of what transpired in 2002.

Ron has taken this project much further than simply chronicling the events surrounding the incident or regurgitating the points of view of those involved. He has reached out to the families and friends of the victims to create a human portrayal of a watershed event that reads more like a novel than a military history book, but it is much more than that. I have often said that losing one's life is the penultimate sacrifice that a person makes for his or her country. The ultimate sacrifice is made by the friends and families of our fallen and disabled heroes, whose lives are irreparably shattered by tragedy and the pain that they have to endure forever. This is an assessment on the Afghan Mission not by politicians and generals, but by some of Canada's so-called "collateral damage" — the people who matter most in information-age warfare.

Canada has the potential to be a global superpower in this world war of influence, but only if we embrace the precept of Sun Tzu's bloodless victories in war. Sergeant Léger, Corporal Dyer, Privates Smith and Green, their comrades, and the tens of thousands of Canadians who followed them to Afghanistan went there to promote the Canadian way of community and self-sacrifice, and to offer the Afghan people a chance to be free of tyranny. Their families were right there beside them, as were all Canadians. Let this book serve as a reminder of how great the cost is, but also how important peace is.

Colonel Pat Stogran, Retired
Former Veterans Ombudsman
Ottawa, Ontario

PROLOGUE

The diner is nearly empty, the lunch crowd long gone. Only one waitress is left working, wiping down tables and folding newspapers.

"This is the *Western Sentinel*, the week after it happened," says Pat Stogran, pushing a newspaper across the table. The front-page photo shows soldiers in maroon berets carrying a metal casket. "It's not a bad story. A lot of the comments made at the time — the governor general, the prime minister — they're all in there.

"Here's *Maclean's* from the same week" — he pushes across a magazine with a banner headline reading "Death by Friendly Fire, What Do We Do Next in Afghanistan?" — "It's a pretty good story. Not all that long. But there are a lot of photos that go with the story."

He keeps rifling through his briefcase, pulling out magazines, newspapers, desk calendars, pushing them across the table toward me. The waitress comes over and says the diner will be closing in fifteen minutes. It is an early morning diner, doesn't stay open past two, even though there was a time when Mello's was open twenty-four hours a day, as busy after the bars and nightclubs closed as it was for breakfast four hours later.

"That was years ago," says the waitress when I ask about the change. "The owner cut the hours as soon as the recession started. Laid off half the staff too."

She walks away and I turn back to the stack of paper in front of me, which grows as Stogran keeps fishing through his briefcase. He looks different from the photographs I have seen of him, both the ones from ten years ago, when he was commander of the first Canadian soldiers sent to Afghanistan, and from two years ago, when he was Canada's Veterans Ombudsman. Not that he's aged so much, he's just different somehow. Maybe it's the unshaven face. Or the herky-jerky animation of the man, which wouldn't come across in photos, of course, especially photos of a stern-looking lieutenant-colonel standing on a runway in Kandahar, or a switchback in the Afghan mountains.

I stare at him, trying to figure out what is different. This is a mental game I will play repeatedly in the next few months, as I interview Canadian soldiers who deployed to Afghanistan in 2002, many of whom I interviewed at the time. Ten years pass and you meet someone again, maybe it's human nature to look for changes, try and calculate what the years have done to that person, how their decade-long journey stacks up against yours. It's a way of keeping score — the planet's winners and losers — a game only seen from a distance, otherwise it's day by day and incremental changes never seem to get tallied.

"This right here," says Stogran, passing over a desk calendar, "this will tell you what the battalion was doing in 2001. A lot of people were away when the shit hit the fan."

I take the calendar and look at the notations. Para Drop (WX). Kapyong 50th. BN Block Leave, B.C., QL4 Basic Recce course. Every day has something noted — a training exercise, a commemoration, an administrative deadline.

I push aside the calendar and start sorting through the other papers stacked in front of me, the front-page photos reminding me of what it was like when Canada lost its first soldiers in Afghanistan. The shock of soldiers dying on a combat mission after forty-nine years of peace-keeping. One-hundred fifty-four deaths later, the stories of dead soldiers started to run on the inside pages of newspapers, closed the first segment of television newscasts, instead of leading. The difference between then and now is right in front of me.

"Will you be speaking to the families?" asks Stogran.

"Yes. Do you keep in touch?"

"Some of them. On Facebook." He shrugs his shoulders and looks momentarily embarrassed. Facebook. It doesn't seem like enough of a connection. "So the book will be all about the friendly fire."

"More than that. I want to tell Léger's story. He didn't have to be there. That's always struck me. And I want to tell the story of the entire deployment, how you ended up in Afghanistan, what everyone is doing today. Where would you start a story like that?"

"At the beginning. September 11."

I nod and he looks away. It occurs to me he might be happier if the book were simply on what happened in Kandahar on April 17, 2002, if it encapsulated that day and nothing more without getting into the messy details of lives that kept rolling.

"Hey, I think I have something else that might help you," he says suddenly, then starts rummaging back through his briefcase, moving around papers and newspapers until he pulls out a plastic-sheathed booklet and slides it across the table. I look at the cover — *CO and RSM Visit Information Package*. Below that is the insignia for the Princess Patricia's Canadian Light Infantry. Below that, the dates August 1–4, 2002.

"When we came back from Afghanistan I visited the families," he says. "That's the booklet that was put together for me."

I open it, the now familiar photos of the four dead soldiers flipping past my eyes. Marc Léger in his maroon beret; Ainsworth Dyer in his jump suit; Nathan Smith, tall and handsome; Ricky Green staring straight at me and trying to look older than his twenty-one years.

"Do you remember the visits?"

"Like it was yesterday. We started in Halifax …"

The waitress interrupts to say the diner is now closed. She's in no hurry, though. She can't get used to finishing work at two in the afternoon. Takes her time going home most days. She refills our coffee cups.

"A guy got your bill before he left. He recognized you" — she points to Stogran — "said to tell you he's got a cousin in the RCR's out in Petawawa. That make sense to you?"

"It does."

"Well, take your time honey."

She walks away and we stir our coffee, the diner now so quiet the clinking of the spoons against our cups seems loud as bells.

"So, you started in Halifax?"

"Yeah. It was a blistering hot day. We flew out of Edmonton and got into Halifax late in the morning. Went right out to Hubbards…."

PART I
Deploy

Never, never, never believe any war will be smooth and easy, or that anyone who embarks on the strange voyage can measure the tides and hurricanes he will encounter. The statesman who yields to war fever must realize that once the signal is given, he is no longer the master of policy but the slave of unforeseeable and uncontrollable events.

— Sir Winston Churchill

A March in the ranks hard-prest and the road unknown
A route through a heavy wood and the muffled steps in the darkness

— Walt Whitman, "A March Through the Ranks Hard-Prest, and the Road Unknown"

CHAPTER ONE

Trondheim, Norway

A harsh light was shining on the Rondane Mountains, the Norwegian dusk still hours away although it was already late afternoon. Lieutenant-Colonel Pat Stogran could clearly make out the footpath running down the western flank of the mountain. He swept his binoculars over the path. There were clearings here and there, places where he could see the A-framed roofline of small houses, wooden fences, cattle.

Team Russia would be somewhere in those mountains. They would want the high ground, and although the exercise could unfold in a thousand different ways — no way of knowing until he got the operation orders next March — it stood to reason that the Russians would be coming from the east and heading straight toward the mountains surrounding Trondheim. From there they would set up artillery positions and make a push for the city and the tenth-century harbour on the southern peninsula of Trondheim Fjord.

He took another sweep with the binoculars. The chestnut and beech trees were in full bloom, although that would be different come March. The Russians would be easy enough to spot then. He wondered again where the NATO line would be positioned, and whether there would be any way of stopping the other team before they took up positions in the mountains. He doubted it. NATO had chosen this city for a reason, and it likely had everything to do with these mountains. What would be the point of having them if you weren't going to use them?

Earlier in the day one of the Canadian commanders had even pulled him aside, and, without giving away the game, had as much as told Stogran he wanted the 3rd Battalion to be ready for "deep recce patrols" during the exercise — which meant they weren't going to be defending shit. Stogran's battalion had the best mountain fighters in the entire Canadian Forces. Each company had trained in the Rockies. The 3rd Battalion trained other countries on how to fight in mountains.

So the Russians would be going in there and his battalion would be tasked with trying to dislodge them. Those would be the orders he'd be looking at next March. He'd bet his pension on it.

He swept the binoculars away from the footpath, looking for the ridges and bluffs where the Russians would set up a forward perimeter. After several minutes of sweeping, looking for high ground in what looked, at this distance, like uniform tree cover, he put down the binoculars and rubbed his eyes. Stogran had arrived in Norway the day before, hadn't adjusted to the time change yet, stayed up way too late the night before, and he'd had a full day on the road. It was starting to catch up to him. He was tired. He was going to make an early night of it. Might even go straight to his room after the Ops briefing back at the hotel.

"What do you say we head back to the hotel," he said to the man standing next to him, Major Peter Dawe.

"Sounds like a plan. You figure they'll be in those mountains somewhere?" said Dawe.

"Don't you?"

The men walked back to their rental car and drove to Trondheim, cutting through a forest with filigreed light, then over the Nidelva River, which was low enough to be showing rocks in the middle channel. Follow the river to the fjord, follow the fjord to its mouth, and you'd be at the Norwegian Sea. Vikings started using Trondheim as a safe harbour as far back as the ninth century, used to call this place the "assembly of free men" because it was where they came to elect their king, right where the river emptied into the fjord, in the safest, most easily defensible position the Vikings knew.

Now NATO would use the town to assemble troops from a dozen countries for Operation Strong Resolve, a simulated exercise that would see an enemy force sweeping into Norway (it wouldn't actually be called Team Russia, it would just come from that direction and use Russian-like weapons) and descend on Trondheim in an attempt to seize the harbour.

It would be the largest military exercise of the year for NATO, and getting ready for it would take up a lot of Stogran's time in the next six months. That and Operation Venturesome Brave, a training exercise with American Rangers scheduled for next month in Fort Lewis, Washington. Two full-battalion exercises in six months. He was thinking of moving a cot into his office.

Dawe drove the car through the streets of Trondheim, both men looking at the wood-framed buildings, most of them painted bright primary colours — red, blue, yellow — the town reminding Stogran of Lunenburg, Nova Scotia. They parked in a lot filled with other rental cars, most of them belonging to the various military advance teams that had come to Trondheim for the week-long recce mission.

Stogran followed Dawe into the hotel, glancing at his watch and seeing that the OPS briefing would be in fifteen minutes, not enough time to go to his hotel room and grab a shower. He walked into the lobby thinking about training exercises and fake Russians, not noticing there was no bellman by the doors, or that the lobby was strangely quiet. There was none of the normal chatter of a busy hotel. No phones ringing. No elevators chiming.

It was only when he walked by the hotel bar that he saw people, a lot of them, crowded inside watching a television. On the screen was an image of the New York City skyline and a plane flying at a strange angle.

What the hell?

Graz, Austria

Master-Corporal Marc Léger and Major Sean Hackett sat at a table and stared at the television screen behind the bar. The television was showing people walking across a bridge over the East River, making their way out of lower Manhattan. They were covered in dirt and dust, many of them glancing back over their shoulder as they marched; whether searching for the twin office towers that had once dominated the skyline, or checking to make sure nothing bad was following them, the two soldiers could not decide.

"It's like they're leaving a war zone," said Léger, taking a sip from his bottle of beer. "Can you believe it?"

Hackett nodded but didn't bother answering. No one in the bar could believe it, although everyone had been watching the same CNN feed for hours now, seen the same images of people fleeing Manhattan, ambulances stuck in rubble-strewn streets, a plane angling itself so it could fly vertically into the South Tower of the World Trade Center, positioning itself for maximum damage, like a defensive tackle turning his body to slip past an offensive guard and rush the blind side of the quarterback.

Deadly skill. The two soldiers recognized it. Admired it in a way others in the bar could not. Whoever was flying that plane was one badass, sumuvabitch.

"This didn't happen overnight," said Hackett, taking a sip of his own beer. "A lot of planning went into an attack like that."

"Do you think it was bin Laden?"

"That's what they're saying. Guess we'll know soon enough."

Hackett was commander of Alpha Company, 3rd Battalion, Princess Patricia's Canadian Light Infantry. A Company was the jump company, a volunteer company of parachutists stationed at the Edmonton Garrison. Hackett was a former member of the disbanded Airborne Regiment and had taken command of the company two months earlier. Commanding an infantry company was something every soldier dreamed of, and getting the jump company added some cachet to the posting. The soldiers in the jump company were considered the best in the battalion.

Léger was typical of a jumper. He stood six-foot-three and weighed 230 pounds. He loved physical training, PT as it was called, and could out-grapple anyone in the company, with the possible exception of a kid from Toronto named Ainsworth Dyer, who competed in Edmonton's Mountain Man competitions, once finishing the course with two fractures in his leg. That kid was tough, but so were all the jumpers.

Eight of them had come to Austria as an advance team for a NATO exercise scheduled for early the next year, but as they stared at the television and drank their beer, both Léger and Hackett were wondering if that was going to happen. The 3rd Battalion was Canada's rapid-deployment force — the proper title was Immediate Reaction Force (Land) — and that plane, well, it looked like it was flying right at them.

Edmonton Garrison

Major Steve Borland had never seen a flash message. Had not been sure such a thing even existed. Perhaps it was a military myth, a legend, like the red phone that supposedly sat on the desk of the president of the United States with the direct line — how would they have wired such a thing in the 1950s? — to the Kremlin. Maybe the hotline existed. Maybe it didn't. He wasn't sure.

A flash message was much the same thing. Talked about but never seen. The highest-possible priority military communications. An order from the upper echelons of National Defence Headquarters that had to be delivered to the recipient as soon as it arrived. Couldn't go into a pending tray. Couldn't wait till the next day. Had to be delivered immediately, whatever it took to make that happen.

A flash message. So it was true.

As second-in-command of the 3rd Battalion, and with Pat Stogran in Norway, the message had made its way to Borland. It was short. One paragraph explaining what had happened in the United States and stating what anyone who had seen the second plane hit the south tower of the World Trade Center already knew. The incident was being treated as an attack against the United States. Enemy unknown.

The second paragraph was even shorter. Canada's Immediate Reaction Force (Land) was to put a company of infantry soldiers on one-hour notice to deploy. The rest of the battalion was to move to forty-eight-hours notice to deploy.

Borland put down the message and let out a quick exhale of breath. Goddamn. This was no duff. This was real. His love of details — a skill others in the battalion found almost spooky — had helped Borland rise quickly through the ranks. As he sat in his office at the 3rd Battalion headquarters, he started using those skills, making a mental list of what needed to be done.

The military police had to be notified, as did the Edmonton Police, to arrange an escort to the airport if they really were bugging out somewhere. The troops had to be notified of the one-hour deployment. That was a problem. Bravo Company was down in Canmore, on a mountain exercise with some British special forces troops. Part of Alpha Company was in Austria. He needed a company to go to one-hour standby but wasn't sure how many soldiers were even on base.

Just do what you can, Steve. Get Bravo back here as quick as possible. They were in the mountains, so it wouldn't be all that quick, but that's how you start.

What else? The regimental quartermaster would have to start pulling some pallets together, get everything a company of light infantry troops would need for, let's say, a three-day deployment. The rest could be shipped to them later.

Transport trucks had to be called up — that needed to go to the top of the list — the trucks had to be checked, fuelled, and marshalled by the front gates. He started writing it down — not that he would be doing the work personally, but he would want to make sure it was getting done. He took his list and the flash message and walked to the office next door, where Glen Zilkalns was sitting. With Peter Dawe over in Norway with Stogran, Zilkalns was the ranking operations officer. Borland couldn't help but smile as he put the papers down on his desk.

"Ever seen a flash message?" he asked.

CHAPTER TWO

It was mere happenstance that put the Patricia's on one-hour notice to deploy on the morning of September 11, 2001. Like much of the rest of this story, there was no logical connection for why such a thing happened, nothing ordained or calculated. It just sort of … happened.

Canada's Immediate Reaction Force (Land) is a military designation that rotates between the 3rd Battalions of Canada's three infantry regiments. One year it might belong to a battalion of the Royal Canadian Regiment in Petawawa, Ontario, Canada's oldest army regiment. Another year it could be the Royal 22nd Regiment, based in Quebec, the fabled Van Doos, given the nickname in the First World War because British army officers kept mispronouncing the name of the Quebec-based regiment — vingt-deux.

But when the terrorist attacks began, and the Edmonton Garrison got a warning order to move a light-infantry company to one-hour-to-deploy status, more than one Patricia's thought there were gremlins at work that morning. Fate conspiring to make an orderly world out of the regular chaos that surrounds us. After all, the regiment's slogan had been "First in Field" since the days of the First World War.

The regiment had been formed in that war, created by Andrew Hamilton Gault, a wealthy Montreal businessman who had served in the 2nd Canadian Mounted Rifles during the Second Boer War. Gault's father, Andrew Frederick Gault, had become rich in the textile business, was called Canada's "King of Cotton" (not the sort of king you normally associate with Canada), and if the family had a tradition of doing things a little differently, Andrew the second would take it to a new level.

Within days of Archduke Ferdinand being assassinated, Gault was boarding a train to Ottawa to pitch the Canadian government on creating a military unit to fight overseas. He offered $100,000 of his own money (two million dollars in today's currency) to fund the unit. On August 6 — two days after Great Britain declared war against Germany — the government accepted Gault's offer, on the condition his money be used to create an infantry unit (Gault had wanted to buy a cavalry unit).

The regiment was named after the daughter of Canada's governor general at the time, the Duke of Connaught, a son of Queen Victoria. Princess Patricia — who became Lady Patricia when she married a commoner in 1919 — had charmed Canadians by showing a surprising love of the country, going on long wilderness treks and once riding a timber crib over the Chaudière Falls. The princess designed the regiment's cap badge and colours from her bedroom at Rideau Hall. The light infantry name came from Gault, who liked the "irregular feel" of the phrase.

The government made the regiment an official Canadian military unit on August 10, 1914, and recruitment began the next day. The fairgrounds in Ottawa were used as the staging area, with people coming from across Canada to enlist, including the Edmonton City Police Pipe Band, which arrived in full highland kilts to announce they were there to pipe the new regiment "to France and back again." Which they did.

Within eight days the regiment had its full complement — 1,098 men, all but forty-nine with previous military experience. They were veterans of the Boer Wars, tough, battle-tested men who were anxious to fight one more time for king and country. The Patricia's sailed for England at the end of August, two months before the rest of the Canadian Expeditionary Force. When the British saw what had landed on their shores, they wasted no time putting the men into the field. Whether out of military logic or self-preservation, no one can quite recall.

The regiment was in France by December, attached to the 80th Brigade Expeditionary Force. On January 8, 1915, Canada suffered its first deaths of the Great War — Lance Corporal Norman Fry and Lance Corporal Henry George Bellinger — two Patricia's. The regiment would see action in every important Canadian campaign of the war — Vimy Ridge to Passchendaele; the Somme to Frezenberg — place names that conjure up images of mud, trench lines, blood, and more blood (the Germans called the Battle of the Somme "das Budblaste" and it remains one of the deadliest conflicts in history — one million casualties and an estimated 200,000 dead on each side).

So impressed was the Canadian government with Gault's army (he served himself, landing in France in 1915 and losing his left leg in battle) that the regiment was kept intact after the war. Even during the Great Depression, when military units were being disbanded across the country, Canada kept a company of Patricia's in Edmonton. When Britain declared war against Germany on September 3, 1939, the Patricia's were brought back up to full strength and again embarked for Europe before any other Canadian soldiers boarded a troop ship.

The regiment did the same thing one more time in Korea, arriving before any other Canadian troops, then taking part in one of the war's greatest battles, the Battle of Kapyong, which pitted the 2nd Battalion of the Patricia's against the vanguard of an entire Chinese division marching its way toward Seoul. During fierce fighting between April 24–25, 1951, on what became known as Hill 677, the Canadians kept the Chinese from advancing down the Kapyong Valley. The battle led to the 2nd Battalion becoming the only Canadian battalion to ever receive the U.S. Presidential Unit Citation for Valour.

Now, as the soldiers of the 3rd Battalion looked at news footage of planes hitting the World Trade Center and read stories about the attack on the Pentagon, they couldn't help but think history was about to repeat itself. Patricia's were going to be First in Field one more time. They just weren't sure which field.

There was one more irony to the Patricia's being put on one-hour notice to deploy, although this one was not a source of regimental pride. The 3rd Battalion was scheduled to disband in two years.

It was part of a Canadian Forces reorganization that would see the light infantry battalions from each of Canada's three infantry regiments be disbanded by 2003. There were two primary reasons for the decision, the first being that in the autumn of 2001 the federal government and the Department of National Defence no longer saw much of a need for light infantry soldiers.

With the end of the Cold War and the generations-long threat of a Soviet ground assault in Europe, many countries felt light infantry soldiers were passé. The dog faces of the Second World War, the dough boys of the Great War — the grunts who used to fight in trenches and march up ridgelines in Italy and France — who needed them? Special forces, high-tech weaponry like predator drones, these were the future of the military. Light infantry was simply a lot of boots on the ground. A lot of costly, old-fashioned, don't-need-them-anymore boots.

The second reason was the Somalia Scandal, perhaps the darkest chapter in the history of the Canadian Forces.

The 1993 fatal shooting of one Somali teenager, and the beating death of another by Canadian soldiers deployed on a United Nation's humanitarian mission in Somalia, had led directly to the disbandment of the Canadian Airborne Regiment and a 25 percent cut in military spending by the federal government. An inquiry into Canada's deployment to Somalia was cut short by the Liberal government in 1997, just months before a general election, but the story would remain in the news for years; a stigma the Canadian Forces could not shake.

By the time of the terrorist attacks in New York City, few of the military leaders so roundly condemned in the Somalia Inquiry's final report were still around. The defence minister was Art Eggleton, who took over the portfolio following the 1997 federal election. The chief of the defence staff was General Ray Henault, a former fighter pilot appointed CDS in June 2001. Still, nearly a decade after the Somalia Scandal broke, many Canadians had begun to mistrust its military and were wondering — outside of responding to natural disasters like floods, fires, and ice storms, or patrolling the country's three coastlines — whether the country even needed the Canadian Forces.

By 2001 some military analysts put the total troop strength of the Canadian Forces at little more than 50,000. In comparison, the country had more than 80,000 troops at the time of the First Gulf War, and at the completion of the Second World War (granted, different circumstances) nearly one million Canadians were in uniform, an almost absurd ratio of one-in-ten Canadians in military service.

Canada had a long and proud military history, from Vimy Ridge to Kapyong, from Egypt to Croatia, but all that history was wiped away by Somalia. Morale in the Canadian Forces was at a historically low level by September 2001. Entire regiments, and now battalions, were being disbanded. Equipment was out of date, sometimes laughably so, good only — or so it seemed some days — for national news reporters to get the occasional front-page news story out of just how bad it was.

Then suddenly, quite unexpectedly, the soldiers were told they were needed.

CHAPTER THREE

On the morning of September 12, Steve Borland left his home for what was normally a ten-minute drive to his office at the Edmonton Garrison, a sprawling military complex home not only to the 3rd Battalion, but also an artillery regiment, an armoured regiment, a combat engineers regiment, and the 1st Battalion of the Princes Patricia's, all part of the 1st Canadian Mechanized Brigade Group. The garrison is also home to Land Force Western Area, the army's operations command centre for Western Canada.

That morning the ten-minute drive took nearly an hour, as Borland hit traffic out on Highway 28, cars backed up trying to get into the main entrance of the garrison. Everyone was getting checked for military identification that day. Didn't matter your rank, didn't matter if you once deployed with the sentry asking for your identification.

Borland had risen early that morning, read the newspaper, watched CNN, the events of the previous day still not registering fully. For the first few seconds after opening his eyes, he wondered if it had been a troubled dream. Then he remembered the trucks lined up and marshalled at the front gate of the garrison, the look on Zilkalns's face when he was given the flash message. It all came back.

Borland was born in Peterborough, Ontario; the son of an accountant who had gone on to start the accounting department at Sir Sandford Fleming College. Just like his father, Borland was good with numbers and small details. It was almost unnerving, his ability to sort things out, keep a big picture and small picture in his head at the same time, adjusting between the two as easily as flipping around the ends of a pair of binoculars.

He didn't come from a military background, but military things had interested him from a young age. It was the logistics of battle as much as anything, troop movement strategy. A good military book was stuffed with the things he liked: details, strategy, big-view stories and little-view stories. When the family went to Germany for a year — his father taking a sabbatical from his college job — Borland had loved going to the sites of famous battles, seeing the places he had read about in his books.

One day, during his senior year at high school, his father brought some university prospectuses and laid them on the coffee table in front of his eldest son. It was time for Borland to decide what he was going to do with his life. The prospectus for Royal Roads Military College practically leapt out of the pile.

His father complimented him on the practicality of the choice. The military would pay for his son's education and give him a good job afterward. A smart decision by a boy who always made smart decisions. When Borland was assigned to an army regiment after graduation, he discovered the choice might have been even smarter than he had suspected. The regiment had a need for people with his skills and passions: organization, logistics. A love of the details many soldiers didn't want to bother with. If it weren't for people like him, military life would be a quagmire.

It was nearly 8:00 a.m. when Borland got through the main gates of the garrison. He drove to the 3rd Battalion headquarters and went to his office, checking on the way there to see if any new warning orders had come in from Ottawa, but none had. There was still a company of light infantry soldiers on one-hour notice to deploy, the rest of the battalion on forty-eight-hours notice. At least B Company had made it back from Canmore. The order was, at least technically, being carried out.

On September 12, 2001, Marc Léger was doing what the rest of the 3rd Battalion was doing back in Edmonton — following news stories, trying to figure out what had happened in New York City the day before, what was going to happen next, trying to concentrate on his work but finding it impossible.

Late that morning he heard about NATO issuing a communiqué condemning the attacks and saying it might invoke Article Five, which stated an attack on one member state was an attack against all, a Cold War-era clause in the NATO treaty that had seemed archaic only two days ago. Later that day someone told him the United Nations had passed something called Resolution 1368, which called on those responsible for the attacks to be held accountable, and reaffirmed the right of member states to self-defence.

To Léger, those were two big all-go signals. Of course, the politicians back in Ottawa were still playing it close to the vest. Prime Minister Chrétien was refusing to say whether NATO and the United Nations had just given a green light for Canada to go to war, but that's how it was adding up in Léger's head. Canadians had been killed in New York. Another had died on one of the hijacked planes, Garnet "Ace" Bailey, a former NHL player. If America was going to hunt down the people who attacked them — and how could they not? — then Canada should go as well. And that meant him, and the rest of the 3rd Battalion. What was the point in being a rapid-deployment force if you didn't deploy for something like Article Five?

He talked to the senior guys in Austria with him, Hackett, Sergeant Lorne Ford, commander of the third platoon's third section, and they read it the same way he did. This wasn't just wishful thinking on his part. After a lifetime of wanting to be a soldier — the no-duff soldier who fought an enemy, who went all in — it looked like that was finally going to happen. He wanted to blow off Austria as fast as he could. Get back to the garrison and start sitting on his rucksack with the rest of the battalion.

Originally from Lancaster, Ontario, Léger had wanted to be a soldier for as long as he could recall. He had joined the Stormont, Dundas and Glengarry Highlanders, a reserve unit, as soon as he was sixteen, and he took it seriously from day one. His mother still teased him about the time a sergeant told him his boots needed to shine so he could see his face in them like a mirror. For two days he'd frantically polished those boots, responding to his mother's pleas to slow down with a panicked: "A mirror, Mom. It's not even close to a mirror yet."

He was earnest like that, a hard-working, serious boy who came from a hard-working, serious family. It had always been that way for the Légers, ever since his great-grandfather had moved to Lancaster from Valleyfield, Quebec, after Lorenzo Léger saved enough money from a slaughter-house job to buy the Commercial Hotel. Léger's great-grandfather had no experience running a hotel, but wanted a better life for his family and he worked hard at making the hotel a success.

Marc Léger was the same stock, a boy who wanted from life what was possible, not what you dreamed about. He was persistent about reaching his goals. Like the time when he was twelve and found an air rifle in one of the sheds at his home. He pestered his dad day and night to go hunting, until finally his dad asked a friend if he could take him. Marc had loved it, although what he bragged about to the other boys at school the next day was not the actual hunt. It was the early morning hike, the way the mist looked on the St. Lawrence, the way the chill of the river soaked through his clothes. Had it still been possible to survive as a guide in Lancaster — as his grandfather had done — Marc might have done that. Instead, he joined the army. And now it looked like he was finally going to get a chance to be a soldier.

Pat Stogran was also anxious to blow off his European training exercise and get back to the Edmonton Garrison. The commander of the 3rd Battalion was an ambitious man — every soldier who makes lieutenant-colonel has hopes of seeing the word *general* in front of their name one day — but there were also times when he figured commanding a light infantry battalion might be about as good as it gets.

He'd been commander for little more than a year. Given that the battalion was going to disband in two years, other commanders might have considered it a caretaker's role — keep everything together until the moving trucks arrive — but not Pat Stogran. The first thing he did when he arrived at the Edmonton Garrison was draft a commanding officer's intent letter, telling his soldiers there was still a place for infantry soldiers and he didn't think their job had changed much from how it had always been defined: "Close with and destroy the enemy in restricted terrain, in all weather, by day and by night."

He wanted them to train hard to reach that goal, take PT seriously; take themselves seriously. Every day he told his troops that light infantry soldiers still had a place in a modern army, that the new emphasis on special forces and digital technology was a mistake. He'd written as much for an article he'd submitted to the *Canadian Army Journal*, which the magazine was considering publishing. The title of the article, "Light Infantry Battalions: The Fledgling Swans of a Joint Force," probably wouldn't make him any friends down at NDHQ, but so what? He still hoped the decision to disband the light infantry battalions could be reversed, and that wasn't going to happen by nodding his head and saying: "Yes, sir."

Stogran was often out with the troops during PT, grabbling along with them, seeing what they could do. He had a black belt in karate and could go up against the biggest man in the battalion. Martial arts had something to do with why he was in the army, a childhood story he liked to tell his troops. Like Borland and Léger, he didn't come from a military family. There was no tradition to continue, no memory in the back of his mind when he walked into the recruiting office and signed the contract. His dad had been a miner, up in Northern Quebec, then had moved the family to Richmond, British Columbia, when he started selling the mining equipment he'd once worked with.

There wasn't a lot to do in Matagami, Quebec, Stogran would tell his soldiers. For fun, he and his brothers sometimes played survival games, dressing up in shorts and T-shirts on a cold winter's day, then head out to the bush to see who could stay outside the longest. In the summer they'd have rock fights with the French kids (his eldest brother fought on both sides, to help balance the teams. A young diplomat-warrior).

Anyway, in that sort of setting you could imagine why any movie playing on television was cause for celebration. And one night the CBC was showing *The Devil's Brigade*. He remembers watching it in the family living room, on an overstuffed couch, hooked from the opening credits. The movie told the story of a Canadian-American special forces commando unit formed during the Second World War — its real name was the 1st Special Service Force — and how the commandos went around blowing up bridges in Italy and France, always working behind enemy lines, or so it was shown in the movie. It starred actors that were big at the time — William Holden, Cliff Robertson, Vince Edwards — and it had plenty of explosions, lots of fights with black-helmeted Nazis, but what Stogran liked best about the movie was one specific scene.

In it the unarmed combat instructor, a Canadian, walked into a room full of big, crazy-as-rabid-bats American soldiers. No one knew the instructor yet, a little guy wearing glasses. The instructor picked a fight with the biggest American in the room. Then tossed him around silly.

For Stogran, who was just starting to be interested in martial arts, that scene was as cool as any Bruce Lee movie. Maybe cooler. Years later, when he enrolled in Royal Roads Military College in Victoria, he told his parents and friends he was doing it because the military was going to give him an education, make him an engineer, but when he was signing the papers, he told his troops years later, he was thinking about *The Devil's Brigade.*

CHAPTER FOUR

Defence Minister Art Eggleton sat in one of the front seats of the Airbus, the cockpit door open, the silence almost eerie. No one on the plane was talking. There was no chatter from the pilots, none of the normal radio signals. It seemed as though this was the only plane making its way across the Atlantic on the night of September 12th.

Chief of the Defence Staff Ray Henault was on the plane with Eggleton; both men reading cables that had arrived at NATO headquarters earlier in the day. Almost two days after the attack on the United States, it was almost certain it had been Osama bin Laden and his group, al Qaeda. The NATO ambassadors had the information when they voted earlier in the day to invoke Article Five, if it turned out the attacks had originated from some-place outside the United States. The qualifier was unnecessary, but it was put in all the same. Perhaps to slow down a story that was moving at a speed the minister had never seen before. It was for situations like this that the word *careening* was invented.

Eggleton and Henault had been in Europe on the morning of September 11th, so they had gone to NATO headquarters for the vote. Neither man thought they would ever see the day Article Five would be threatened, not seriously anyway, and certainly not after the collapse of the Soviet Union. The next few days were going to be a serious test for both of them.

Eggleton, the former mayor of Toronto, had been defence minister for more than four years, replacing Doug Young when Young had been defeated in the 1997 general election. The former minister was one more casualty of what the press still loved to call the Somalia Scandal. The Canadian Forces had been in the Balkans, in some sort of way, for all of Eggleton's tenure as defence minister, and Canada was part of the NATO campaign in Kosovo as well, something he had lobbied for, so the politics of military deployments would be nothing new for him.

As for Ray Henault, this was going to be new territory. The former fighter pilot is a soft-spoken man — Eggleton had to crane his neck to hear him sometimes during meetings — and you probably would guess he was air force without even being told, as he is not a large man. He has the diminutive stature that benefits fighter pilots, who have to be crammed into a cockpit for hours on end. He had worked his way up the ranks without so much as a misstep, becoming chief of the defence staff two-and-a-half months earlier.

It would be baptism by fire for the general, although experience might not count for much in this situation. The prime minister had already informed Eggleton that a new cabinet committee was being formed to respond to the events of September 11, an ad hoc committee that would consist of the ministers of justice, transport, defence, foreign affairs, the solicitor general, and the deputy prime minister. It hadn't even had its first meeting yet, hadn't even been given a name, but it was already the most powerful cabinet committee on the Hill. A non-budgetary committee having that much clout was unheard of — the world had indeed changed in less than a day.

Eggleton leaned back and looked out the window at a starless night with no visible clouds; black as an oil spill. He wondered when the United States would make a formal request for military support, and what they would be looking for.

When Eggleton and Henault landed at CFB Uplands later that night, they would disembark to a political maelstrom.

The Department of National Defence was virtually under siege by reporters clamouring for information — any information — on what the Canadian Forces were doing in the wake of the terrorist attacks. Opposition leaders were already saying Canada was not doing enough to support the United States, and they weren't the only critics of the government. Some military analysts and former commanders were saying there would not be much the country could do to help the United States, even if it wanted to, so deep and wide-ranging had the cuts in military spending been under the Chrétien government.

This three-front attack — the media on one front asking: "What are you doing?" Pundits on the second front asking: "Can you do anything?"

Opposition politicians on the third saying: "You're not doing enough" — would continue like an aerial barrage over the heads of the defence minister and the chief of the defence staff for the rest of the year.

On the political front, Prime Minister Chrétien was being criticized for saying, "There is no discussion at this time of any specific action," when reporters had asked him how Canada would respond to the NATO and UN votes. Leader of the official opposition, Stockwell Day, said the comment fell far short of unequivocal support for the United States. "This is clearly a barbaric attack on Canada as well," said Day. "We urge the prime minister to unequivocally offer Canadian military support to the United States in any actions they might undertake."

When asked similar questions about Canada's possible military response by reporters, Bill Rodgers, a spokesman for Conservative leader Joe Clark, said, "We want to know the facts first and then we'll make the decision." Bloc Quebecois foreign affairs critic Francine Lalonde said it was "irresponsible" to be talking about military action until it was proven who the terrorists were.

As for the New Democratic Party, there appeared to be dissension in the ranks. Its foreign affairs critic, Svend Robinson, was saying Canada should "not sign a blank cheque" for support of American-led military action, while defence critic Peter Stoffer said Canada should be part of any military action "short of nuking them."

After politicians took the first swing at the ball, military analysts began wading in with their opinions on the terrorist attacks and what Canada's response should be. Sean Henry, a retired Canadian Forces officer with the Conference of Defence Associations, sent out a press release telling reporters Canada did not have the troop strength to sustain even a minor contribution to any war on terror. "There is some capacity," said Henry, "but it is a minor capacity and it would not be possible to maintain it past six months."

At National Defence Headquarters people were scrambling to deflect the criticism. Reporters were briefed on what the military had already done in response to the terrorist attacks. They were told that on September 11, Canadian Hercules aircraft had flown blankets and cots from Ottawa to Halifax to help the thousands of American airline passengers stranded when airports across the United States were shut down. Troops from

Canadian Forces Base Gagetown had also been ferried to Gander, Newfoundland, to help aircraft passengers diverted there.

The rest of the Canadian Forces had been placed on a "heightened state of readiness." The order to increase deployment readiness had come directly from the prime minister. Some light infantry companies had been placed on one-hour notice to deploy, the reporters were told, ready to respond immediately to any task that was given them, although no one knew what that task might be.

CHAPTER FIVE

Steve Borland made his way around the 3rd Battalion headquarters building. He wanted to see how the troops were responding to the one-hour deployment notice. Check on the work being done. He found the regimental quartermaster, Wayne Green, in the storeroom on the main floor. He had a clipboard in his hand and was staring at a pallet of MREs, Meals Ready to Eat — although the troops who have to eat the dehydrated meals often have other phrases for the acronym, Meals Ready to Explode being one of the most common.

"What time did you finish yesterday?" Borland asked him.

"'Bout one in the morning," Green answered.

"How do you think we're sitting?"

"Depends where we're going. Have you heard anything?"

"Not a word. Get ready for anything, I guess."

"Well, what we've got stored is on pallets. 'Bout all I can do right now."

Green had wanted to join a tank battalion when he enlisted, but couldn't master some of the exercises, so he'd been assigned to logistics when he graduated from Royal Military College. He was surprised when he didn't mind the work. It was challenging, kept his mind busy. He would never know what it would be like to be in combat as a tank gunner, but what he had just been through in the storeroom since yesterday morning — getting an infantry battalion ready to deploy to God knows where — it had been an adrenaline rush. There was no other way to describe it.

Borland left Green and went outside to check on the trucks marshalled by the front gates, several with the hoods popped open and mechanics underneath poking around, no doubt checking the fluids, the belts, the plugs. Where the trucks could be going — where the pallets would be going, for that matter — was a good question. He had heard on the radio before leaving his office that the airspace across North America was still shut down. But you couldn't think these things through too much, get ahead of yourself. Just get ready and let others decide what came next.

He walked back into the battalion headquarters and into the canteen, where soldiers were sitting at tables, eyes riveted to a television turned to CNN. He stood and watched — it was hard to turn your eyes away from a television that day — and learned the United Nations had just passed Resolution 1368. NATO was threatening Article Five. He left the canteen and went back upstairs, going into Glen Zilkalns office before returning to his own.

"So we're still on one-hour notice to deploy," said Zilkalns, rolling up a newspaper and flipping it to the corner of his desk.

"That's right. You're ready to ship out, aren't you?"

"Oh yeah. Let me get my toothbrush."

Zilkalns was a kindred soul; another details man who loved the military. The two men spoke for a while about the one-hour notice to deploy, both agreeing it was as plausible as Osama bin Laden walking into Zilkalns's office that very minute and apologizing for what he'd done. Until the terrorist attacks, the battalion had been on seventy-two hours to deploy, and that meant you needed that time just to change your operational status. You didn't jump from three days to one hour with the issuing of a press release. Details like that — the sheer, obvious stupidity of saying an army unit was now on one-hour-standby, in fact, telling the media that — it drove Zilkalns crazy.

"Have you heard anything new?" he asked.

"From Ottawa?"

"Yeah."

"Nothing. Expect we might get some sort of update later today."

Borland left Zilkalns and went back to his office. On his desk was a note saying Pat Stogran had called. The commander was looking for an update.

While Stogran waited to hear from Borland, he cursed his luck, being stuck in Norway while his battalion was in Edmonton on one-hour notice to deploy. From what he had seen on television, what he had read in the newspapers, Canada's rapid-deployment force could end up as part of a combat mission. The no-duff mission where you weren't handcuffed by warm fuzzy rules of engagement that left you watching as people were murdered around you. This could be a mission where soldiers did what soldiers were supposed to do — fight the bad guys — and people who weren't soldiers benefitted because of it.

He had already been on the other sort of mission — the peacekeeping mission where you observed a one-sided war and couldn't stop it — and it still rankled, still left a bad, dank taste in his mouth. Nearly destroyed his career as well.

In 1994, thirty-four-year-old Major Pat Stogran was a rising star in the Canadian Forces. He had already been a section commander, a platoon commander, had been given the short stints a young officer gets assigned to when he's being groomed for bigger things — NDHQ, the Staff College in Toronto. In April of that year he was given another plum assignment, chosen to be a United Nations military observer in Goražde, a small city in southeastern Bosnia.

Within a week of arriving to take up his post, United Nations military forces pulled out of Goražde, leaving Stogran and a handful of civilian aid workers behind. Almost as soon as the British SAS troops left, the Bosnian-Serb army started an artillery assault on the predominately Muslim city.

Despite the sustained Serbian offensive, the United Nation's military commander in Bosnia at the time, British General Michael Rose, kept telling the United Nations there was little fighting going on in Goražde. Stogran would see the United Nation's cables, hear the BBC world reports, and wonder if everyone was talking about the same village he was hiding in.

To prove how absurd the reports were, Stogran began venturing out at night. He went with a local Bosnian interpreter, the two men prowling the streets and taking photos of people lying in hospital beds, a makeshift cemetery in the middle of town, the damage left from heavy artillery fire. After several nights of nocturnal wanderings, Stogran filed a report, faxing it to a general-delivery UN number that would automatically forward to various delegations and media outlets. The next day the BBC (as well as the CBC and National Public Radio in the United States) reported that Goražde, a supposedly safe city under UN protection, was under siege by the Serbian army.

General Rose was outraged. He said publicly that Stogran's report was inaccurate, exaggerated, and that the task of impartial United Nations military observer seemed beyond his capabilities. Privately, Rose railed on about the young major's insubordination. Within days, however, the United Nations issued an ultimatum to the Serbs, telling them to stop shelling the city or get prepared for an air assault on their positions surrounding Goražde. When the shelling stopped, Stogran, the aid workers, and many wounded civilians were airlifted to Sarajevo.

Far from being complimented, back in Canada Stogran was shunned. While never formally reprimanded, he was told privately that embarrassing a British general was not the wisest career move a Canadian army major could make. A career counsellor at National Defence Headquarters told him his career was effectively finished. He would never receive another promotion. Never get command of anything large than a company of infantry soldiers. Privately, Stogran started making plans to pension out after twenty-five years.

Then an out-of-the-blue thing happened. ABC news anchor Peter Jennings had heard about Stogran's report and invited him to New York City to talk about Goražde. Figuring his career was over and he had nothing to lose, Stogran agreed to go.

The ABC special report that Jennings subsequently aired was called "The Failure of Bosnia," and it rewrote the official record on what happened in the Balkans while under United Nations protection. (It is now generally agreed that 700 people died in Goražde during the Serb offensive, while another 2,000 were wounded.)

Suddenly Stogran's reputation was restored. Perhaps his commanding officers had been right at the outset, when they thought an independent, no-duff army major was what was required in Bosnia. In an act of almost contrition, Stogran was promoted to lieutenant-colonel and given command of the 3rd Battalion.

Now, with his battalion on one-hour standby and Article 5 being threatened by NATO, he was stuck in Norway, training to go after fake Russians. One more time, he cursed his bad luck.

* * *

Marc Léger was also going through the motions in Austria, pretending his exercise still mattered, but fairly convinced it was never going to happen. He phoned his wife as often as he could to get updates on what was happening back home.

Marley Léger could tell her husband was excited at the thought of going on a combat mission, although he wouldn't come right out and say it. It was typical of him — he used to apologize for having to go on lengthy training missions, then almost skip onto the bus carrying his rucksack.

She had met Marc when she was sixteen. He was two years older and played on the defensive line of the Cornwall Wildcats, a junior football team that won its first three games of the 1991 season, prompting someone on the team to organize a party.

Marc was outside throwing a football when Marley arrived at the party with a friend. Marc threw her the football, she caught it, threw it back, and never made it inside the house, just stood outside the rest of the night throwing a football. On the drive home, she told her friend she had just met the man she was going to marry. The friend laughed and said she was crazy.

But the next week Marc called and asked her to go on a date. He took her to dinner, the two of them driving in an old Toyota with the windows down, the cool autumn air rushing through the car so that Marley's dark hair got blown into a tangled mess.

"So, tell me about yourself," he said.

"What do you want to know?"

"Everything."

And so she told him: two younger brothers who were always in her hair. Her mother was a school teacher, her father ran a vending machine and catering business in Cornwall. She wasn't sure what she would do when she finished school. Maybe go to St. Lawrence College to earn a business degree. She liked working in an office, was pretty good with numbers and math, so it made sense.

"Do you know what you want to do after school?" she asked.

"I'm thinking of joining the army."

"That sounds exciting."

"It will be."

They hurried through their supper so they could get back into their car and continue driving, continue talking, until they realized they were late, and Marc had to escort her to the front door to explain to her father. By the following week, they were boyfriend and girlfriend.

Marc enlisted one year later, and Marley went with him to the recruiting office in Ottawa. Two weeks later they were back driving the Toyota down country roads, his last night as a civilian.

"How is this going to work?" Marley asked.

"I don't know, but we'll find a way."

"But how? I'm never going to see you."

"I'm joining the army. Not going to the moon."

A light snow was falling and a full moon lit up the St. Lawrence, its shore ringed by ice; dark, blue water moving slowly through the middle of the channel. Marley stared out the car window and began to cry.

"You really think this can work?"

"It can if we love each other."

"And we do, right?"

"We do."

The next morning he boarded a train for Cornwallis, NS, to begin his basic training. He was nineteen.

That seemed a long time ago, but whenever Marley looked at her husband, or talked to him when he was on a mission or deployment overseas, she still remembered the good-looking teenage football player who threw her a football more than a decade ago.

"You're excited about maybe going on a combat mission, aren't you, Marc?" she said.

"No, I'm not."

"Marc," she said sternly.

"All right, babe, maybe just a little."

CHAPTER SIX

On September 14th the federal government declared an official day of mourning for the victims of the terrorist attacks in the United States. While there were rallies held across the country that Friday, the largest was in Ottawa, where an estimated 100,000 people went to Parliament Hill.

Security was tight, with RCMP officers checking the bags of some people walking through the gates onto the grounds of the Parliament Buildings. Sniffer dogs trotted through the throng. Police snipers could be seen on the rooftops of nearby buildings. The RCMP had suggested holding the rally indoors, in order to have even more security, but Prime Minister Chrétien insisted on an outdoor event.

Standing in front of the Parliament Buildings with the prime minister that day was Governor General Adrienne Clarkson and American Ambassador Paul Cellucci, who thanked all Canadians, and the military specifically, for all they had done since the attacks. "You truly are," said the ambassador, "our closest friends."

Before the ambassador spoke there was three minutes of silence, followed by a somber tolling of the Peace Tower carillon. As the bells rang, three balloons were released — one red, one white, one blue — to float over the crowd and then disappear behind the Gatineau Hills. Both the American and Canadian anthems were sung by an Ontario Provincial Police officer, a thunderous round of applause followed.

When it was his time to speak, Chrétien looked directly at Cellucci and said, "We have travelled many difficult miles together, side by side. We have lived through many dark times, always firm in our shared resolve to vanquish any threat to freedom and justice, and together with our allies we will defy and defeat the threat that terrorism poses to all civilized nations."

As the crowd applauded, Chrétien added: "Mr. Ambassador, we will be with the United States every step of the way, as friends, as neighbours, as family."

For many in the crowd, Chrétien's comments were heard as heartfelt rhetoric. Well-crafted sentences bespeaking the horror of the week, and a determination to overcome adversity.

For soldiers in the 3rd Battalion of the Princess Patricia's Canadian Light Infantry, many of whom watched the rally in the base canteen, there was a more practical take on the speech. They were left wondering what the prime minister had meant, exactly, by "every step of the way."

Events moved quickly after that. The same day as the official day of mourning, the one-hour notice to deploy order was rescinded and the battalion went back to seventy-two-hour standby. Hurry up and wait. There is a good reason that is a military maxim.

Like the rest of the country, the soldiers spent the next few weeks working, while at the same time trying to follow the latest developments of what American President Bush was calling a "war on terror." If anything, the soldiers had more time on their hands than normal, as the full-battalion exercise planned for October with American Rangers at Fort Lewis, Washington, had been cancelled.

On September 20th the United States government issued a formal demand to the Afghanistan government to hand over all resident al Qaeda members, including Osama bin Laden, and close all terrorist training camps. The same day, Defence Minister Eggleton authorized Canadian Forces members on exchange assignments in the United States and other allied nations to participate in operations responding to the September 11 attacks. Eggleton would tell reporters this represented about a hundred Canadian Forces personnel.

The next day the Afghanistan government refused the United Sates ultimatum, calling it a form of aggression and saying it doubted there was solid information linking bin Laden to the terrorist attacks. The following week the United Nations passed Resolution 1373, which set out methods for identifying and rooting out terrorist organizations and cutting off their funding.

On October 3, UN Secretary-General Kofi Annan appointed Algerian diplomat Lakhdar Brahimi to the position of special representative of the secretary-general for Afghanistan. Brahimi met with Taliban ministers, who offered to put bin Laden on trial if the United States turned over evidence linking him to the terrorist attacks. The U.S. dismissed the offer.

The following day, saying it was satisfied bin Laden was the architect of the September 11 terrorist attacks and that the attacks were planned in terrorist camps in Afghanistan, NATO invoked Article Five. It was the first time the attack-on-one-member-is-an-attack-on-all clause had been used.

Three days later, on October 7, the United States and Great Britain began Operation Enduring Freedom. It was the official start of the war in Afghanistan and it began with air strikes against al Qaeda and Taliban targets in Kabul, Kandahar, and Jalalabad, shortly after 3:00 p.m. Eastern Standard Time. Soldiers in the 3rd Battalion gathered in the canteen to watch a television tuned to CNN, which was broadcasting exclusive footage of Kabul under attack. Most of the soldiers stayed in the mess until Prime Minister Chrétien delivered a short televised address to the nation later that day.

On Sept. 11, 2001, Canada and the world looked on in shock and disbelief as the deadliest terrorist attack in history was carried out against thousands of defenceless victims in New York and Washington.

This was an act of premeditated murder on a massive scale with no possible justification or explanation — an attack not just on our closest friend and partner, the United States, but against the values and the way of life of all free and civilized people around the world.

From the moment of the attack, I have been in close communication with President George Bush, who has been a symbol to the world of calm, courage, resolve and wisdom. I told him that Canada stands shoulder to shoulder with him and the American people. We are part of an unprecedented coalition of nations that has come together to fight the threat of terrorism. A coalition that will act on a broad front that includes military, humanitarian, diplomatic, financial, legislative and domestic security initiatives.

I have made it clear from the very beginning that Canada would be part of this coalition every step of the way.

On Friday evening, the United States asked Canada to make certain contributions as part of an international military coalition against international terrorism.

I immediately instructed our minister of national defence to agree. Yesterday, I met with the chief of the national defence staff to confirm the type of role that Canada was being asked to play. And shortly before noon today, I confirmed to President Bush in a telephone conversation that we would provide the military support requested.

Just after noon, I instructed the chief of defence staff to issue a warning order to a number of units of our Armed Forces to ensure their readiness.

All Canadians understand what is being asked of the men and women of our Armed Forces and their families. As always, they are ready to serve. As always, they will do Canada proud. I have spoken as well to the leaders of opposition parties. They pledged their co-operation and I thank them for it.

While I obviously will not be able to provide the Canadian people with operational information that could endanger lives, I intend to offer regular updates on our objectives and efforts. I will meet with my cabinet this week and a take-note debate will be held in Parliament on Monday of next week.

We will also be introducing a series of programs and legislative steps to deal with the threat of terrorism.

I would like to thank all the Canadians who have worked around the clock to come to the aid of our American friends in their time of need. I have made clear in the days since September 11 that the struggle to defeat the forces of terrorism will be a long one. We must remain strong and vigilant. We must insist on living on our terms, according to our values not on terms dictated from the shadows.

I cannot promise that the campaign against terrorism will be painless, but I can promise that it will be won. Thank you.

The next day's newspapers carried banner headlines CANADA AT WAR. Eggleton and Henault held a press conference at National Defence Headquarters to explain exactly what the headlines meant, and what Canada had agreed to contribute to Operation Enduring Freedom. The Canadian military operation was given its own codename, Operation Apollo, and in addition to an undisclosed number of commandoes from Joint Task Force 2 (JTF2), the frigate HMCS *Halifax* would be deployed immediately to the Persian Gulf. It had 230 sailors and was with NATO's Standing Naval Force Atlantic.

In addition to the *Halifax*, more than a thousand navy personnel would be deployed from Halifax. The Air Force would be sending three Hercules, one Airbus, and two Aurora Maritime patrol aircraft. All of this was an open-ended commitment, but the initial deployment was expected to last six months. The total commitment of troops was roughly two thousand. Ground troops were not part of the deployment.

"At the moment, the United States has not requested ground troops," explained Henault.

"Could that change?" asked a reporter.

"Yes, that could change," he answered. "If the American make a formal request for ground troops, that is something we would consider at that time."

CHAPTER SEVEN

The next three months would be a test of the patience and good humour of every soldier in the 3rd Battalion. While it is easy to remember the autumn of 2001 as an inexorable march toward the deployment of Canadian soldiers into Afghanistan, the public record shows it was not.

What follows is a short chronology of the press conferences, press releases, official statements, scrums, Hansard entries, and interviews that make up that record.

Ten days after the prime minister's televised address to the nation, Chrétien, Eggleton, and Henault go to Halifax, where a naval band plays "Hearts of Oak" while three Canadian warships sail out of Halifax Harbour, bound for the Arabian Sea. Thousands of people line the waterfront to see the ships — HMCS *Iroquois*, HMCS *Charlottetown*, and HMCS *Preserver* — steam out of port.

The prime minister's farewell speech, "I say to you on your departure, Bravo Zulu," may still have been ringing in the sailor's ears when, less than a week later, Conservative MP Elsie Wayne sent out a press release saying the sailors left Halifax without chemical and biological weapons suits. When asked about the allegation, Eggleton refuses to comment specifically, but hints the suits may be delivered to the sailors en route.

"What's important is that they have all of what they need," says the minister. "I'm not talking about anything specific here, but that they have all that they need when they get into the theatre of operations."

On November 13th Northern Alliance soldiers march into Kabul and the Taliban government falls. Two days later, the 3rd Battalion is put on forty-eight-hours notice to deploy. Eggleton tells reporters the soldiers might be deployed as early as the following week, to join a multinational, British-led force in Afghanistan.

At the Edmonton Garrison, soldiers roll up their sleeves to get inoculation shots. Speculation is they are on their way to Kabul, or the northern city of Herat. An advance party from the battalion flies to Ottawa for final briefings on the mission. The advance party is told it will not be returning to the garrison, but will fly directly to Afghanistan.

Four days later, Eggleton tells reporters the advance party is back in Edmonton and the 3rd Battalion is being taken off forty-eight-hour notice. The turnabout happens after Northern Alliance troops open fire on a British advance team when it arrives in Kabul.

"We obviously have a number of things still to work out," says Eggleton. "The Northern Alliance response to the British going in is a factor ... obviously, we're not going to send our people into a condition in which they're unwelcome."

In the House of Commons, Prime Minister Chrétien adds: "Of course we do not want to have a big fight there. We want to bring peace and happiness as much as possible."

The opposition parties take the government to task over the about-face, complaining that Canada's military plan is still unclear, six weeks after the prime minister has committed the country to military action in Afghanistan. Did the defence minister's "unwelcome" comment mean Canada would not be sending combat troops? Would we be sending "peace and happiness" troops instead?

In an apparent attempt to quiet the rising chorus of criticism, on December 5th Eggleton's office says soldiers with JTF2 are being deployed to Afghanistan. The next day, 3PPCLI is again told they could be in Afghanistan before Christmas. The mission has changed, though. This time, the soldiers will be part of an "international peacekeeping force" the U.S. has been pushing to create.

One week later, the soldiers in Edmonton are told the mission has changed yet again. The Americans are out. The Brits are back in. The Northern Alliance has agreed to allow foreign troops into Kabul, and the British have asked for Canadian soldiers to go in with them. When news of the agreement is made public, media reports say Canadian troops could be in Afghanistan within days.

One week later, the troops are again told to stand down. This time the change in operational status is blamed on the United Nations, which has decided to pass a resolution on what the composition and mandate should be of any security force sent to Afghanistan. Chrétien tells reporters it could be "several weeks" before such a resolution is passed, and several weeks after that before any Canadian troops are deployed.

The next day, after the most recent stand-down order, Eggleton tells reporters JTF2 troops have arrived in Afghanistan. They are operating around Kandahar. And after more than three months of talking, debating, and posturing about sending ground troops to Afghanistan, the defence minister also tells reporters how many Canadian soldiers are in theatre: forty.

If the public record seems confusing, the situation at the Edmonton Garrison was worse. Soldiers would read the news stories coming out of Ottawa and ask their platoon or section commanders if they were true, the commanders would ask Stogran, and the battalion commander would say he knew as much as they did.

Years later, both Eggleton and Henault would say part of the problem was a desire by the federal government to make a "meaningful contribution" to the military operations going on in Afghanistan. Prime Minister Chrétien wanted to send a battle group to Afghanistan, and requests by the British to send Canadian engineers to Kabul, or administrative and logistical personnel to help the Americans, were rejected. Nor was there any interest in pursuing an idea floated by American Ambassador Paul Cellucci, who suggested sending Canadian troops to the Balkans to "backfill" for American troops stationed there, so the Americans could be deployed to Afghanistan.

In hindsight, the four-month delay in deploying ground troops might have been a good thing. Getting soldiers into theatre is a logistical challenge at the best of times; preparing for a combat deployment, on short notice, is the same sort of challenge, to the power of ten. The two soldiers who bore much of the responsibility for getting the battalion ready to deploy were Wayne Green and Glen Zilkalns.

Right after Operation Apollo began, Zilkalns began making a list of the equipment and troops that would likely be needed for a combat mission in Afghanistan. There was extra urgency to this task as the Canadian Forces had recently changed its tracking and inventory software. The new program was called the Joint Expedition Materials

Management System (JEMMS), a proprietary system created solely for the Canadian Forces.

Zilkalns had to take all the information stored on Microsoft Excel spreadsheets and convert it to JEMMS spreadsheets. What would have been a laborious task to begin with was made more so because the two software programs were not compatible. Zilkalns had to print off the Excel spreadsheets and manually input the data on a different computer. The job took months.

When it finally came time to deploy, the battle group was airlifted into Afghanistan on American C-5 transport planes. The Americans had never heard of JEMMS. They asked Zilkalns if he could covert the information to Excel.

Vehicles were a similar muddle. Because the 3rd Battalion was a light infantry unit, it drew vehicles from a transportation pool at the garrison, or from other battalions or regiments. The battalion couldn't wait until the last minute to put in a request, but because the deployment to Afghanistan was an unknown, they didn't know what sort of vehicles would be needed. So they started to assemble everything at the garrison that had wheels and fossil-fuel propulsion. Other bases started shipping vehicles as well, their poor quality leading Zilkalns to suspect some transportation pools were getting rid of trucks and Jeeps they no longer wanted. By Christmas, some soldiers on the base were saying the Guinness Book of Records should be contacted, to see if the Edmonton Garrison was now in possession of the world's longest linear parking lot.

And then there was the toilet paper. A story that should tell you everything you need to know about how prepared Canada was to go on its first combat mission in forty-nine years.

When the 3rd Battalion was told to put a company on one-hour notice to deploy on the morning of September 11, there was an immediate problem. It wasn't just that the commander was in Norway. Or that a lot of the soldiers were in the mountains of southern Alberta. The biggest problem was the pallets. Shipping pallets are the bone-and-marrow of a modern army. Soldiers ship out with their rucksacks and weapons; everything else they need follows on pallets. A true rapid-deployment force should have shipping pallets assembled and ready to go. That's what the Airborne Regiment used to do. The regiment even practised a drill — a quick-rig drill it was called — to see how fast it could get pallets from Canadian Forces Base Petawawa to the Trenton Air Base.

At the Edmonton Garrison it took Wayne Green an entire day just to get pallets ready to ship, let alone getting them onto trucks and then onto an airplane. It wasn't his fault. There had never been a directive from NDHQ to replicate the quick-rig drills of the Airborne Regiment. Once the pallets were assembled, Green also saw that some items were missing. Stuff that wasn't in the warehouse — like collapsible ladders — that would be needed on a combat mission. He put in a request for the missing items.

But in mid-November, when the battalion was put on forty-eight hours to move, the "consumables" had yet to arrive. Consumables are items like bottled water, paper towels, and … toilet paper. Thinking the soldiers were on their way to Afghanistan in two days, Green had to solve this problem quickly. So he sent soldiers to a store in Edmonton to purchase toilet paper and bottled water for Canada's rapid-deployment force.

It was a Shoppers Drug Mart that the soldiers went to, purchasing everything on the store shelves, and then additional supplies that were shipped from the company's warehouse. The soldiers put the purchases on military credit cards and, when they went over the limit, had the store manager invoice the battalion for the remainder.

The soldiers dispatched to the Shoppers Drug Mart didn't ask a lot of questions — "We'll take everything you've got on the shelves" — and this was particularly true for one consumable item. As Green would recall years later: "If you're a man, how many brand names do you know for feminine hygiene products? The guys went into the store and just froze. Said they'd take whatever the store had. Didn't even want to see them."

CHAPTER EIGHT

NATO Permanent Joint Headquarters, Northwood, U.K.

Pat Stogran looked around the meeting room and felt silly. While members of the other military delegations were in their parade uniforms, medals glinting from their chests, he was dressed in camouflage. He wished he had brought his uniform, but he hadn't been expecting so many meetings; so many days spent in the NATO complex known as Northwood, so named because it was situated just outside the London suburb of the same name.

When he had left Ottawa after his briefings at NDHQ a couple days before, he had been expecting a quick trip to Northwood, then right onto a plane for Afghanistan. He had brought what he would need for Afghanistan: his kit, his C-7 rifle, his pistol — and his camouflage. He didn't have a lot of space for parade uniforms, wouldn't need them in Afghanistan, so he had left them behind, a decision he now regretted.

Unlike the advance party that went to Ottawa in November — shortly after Kabul had fallen, the last time he was expecting to fly to Afghanistan — Stogran was the only soldier from the Edmonton Garrison on this trip to England. The rest of the Canadian delegation was officers permanently assigned to Northwood, some foreign affairs people, some senior-ranks people from NDHQ, and Stogran, sitting there in his "camos" and feeling like the Jolly Green Giant.

The meetings were being chaired by the British, who were finally going to go into Kabul, since the Northern Alliance had agreed to allow NATO ground troops into the capital. When the Northern Alliance had started shooting at a British advance team, back in November, that's when the first advance party from the Edmonton Garrison had been sent home. Now, a month later, the deployment was back on.

Stogran had been briefed back in Ottawa on the mission, and he could already imagine the groans he was going to hear from the soldiers when they arrived in Kabul. The Canadians would be maintaining a security perimeter around the airfield, and escorting dignitaries around Kabul. This was not going to be a combat mission.

When he first arrived at Northwood, Stogran had been shown where the battalion was going to be deployed, where the Canadian base was going to be, and where the security line around the airfield would be. The map was already drawn, and he thought it would be a quick visit, but the briefing meetings had dragged on. He listened to British army officer after British army officer explain to the military delegations that they wanted to be in Kabul for only a few months to "stabilize the situation," then they wanted to hand the mission over to another country. They were looking for a battle group that would let them bug out early in the New Year. As Stogran listened he realized this was a task far beyond what he had been briefed on before leaving Canada, or when he had arrived at Northwood. Confused, he sat through two days of briefings, the Brits dropping hint after hint that they had a ball they wanted to throw to someone, until finally a Turkish army officer in full parade uniform stood up and offered to take over from the British within six weeks of arriving in theatre.

"My Lord," thought Stogran, "that's a hell of an offer. What are they going to need us for?"

He stayed in Northwood for two more days, not party to discussions between the NDHQ officers and their U.K. counterparts, as the Brits explained what the Canadians could still contribute. They didn't want Canadian soldiers. They wanted engineers, medics, some support and logistics personnel. The requests were forwarded to Eggleton and Henault back in Canada, then on to the prime minister, who turned down the British request.

"The British wanted to take bits and pieces from our battle group," Eggleton would explain years later. "Some medics here, some engineers there. It wasn't the sort of contribution we were looking to make. It wasn't a meaningful contribution."

Henault would remember the British wanting primarily Canadian engineers — "as many as two hundred" — and agreed with Eggleton that this was not a worthwhile contribution. The Canadian government wanted to send a battle group.

After nearly a week in Northwood, Stogran received orders to return to Canada. For the second time in two months, he wasn't going to be flying on to Afghanistan after all. He flew back on a commercial flight and landed at MacDonald-Cartier International Airport in Ottawa on December 22, where he was scheduled to have a quick meeting at NDHQ before continuing on to Edmonton. The airport was crowded with holiday travellers. There was a long line at customs. When Stogran got to the window he was asked why he was carrying a pistol and an assault rifle.

He would be held in an interrogation room for six hours, until customs officials were able to verify they were detaining the commander of Canada's rapid-deployment force.

The 3rd Battalion Christmas party in 2001 was held in the hangar at the Edmonton Garrison, the large garage done up with Christmas garlands and lights, plastic tablecloths with strands of holly running along the edges spread out on the tables.

The party started with Stogran and the youngest private in the battalion exchanging tunics, the private becoming the battalion's commanding officer for the night, Stogran busted down to private. After a short speech welcoming the new commanding officer, dinner was served: turkeys were wheeled out on carts and served table to table. There was stuffing to go with the turkey, roasted vegetables, plum pudding for dessert. Throughout the dinner the young private was goaded and teased into making announcements from the head table, things along the lines of: "A warning order will be coming shortly from NDHQ — we are being deployed to Calgary."

Marc Léger sat with the rest of his company, enjoying the skits going on at the head table. The presentation of the Horse's Ass Award for the team that had lost the hockey game played earlier in the day at the garrison's sports complex (it was the officers). And the speeches from the private turned CO, who would regret a few things the next day if he didn't ratchet it down a notch. It was a lucky thing for him there was a two-beer ration for the party. No one in the room was going to benefit from that order more than the private.

As much fun as he was having, Léger was looking forward to going home, where Marley was waiting. His wife was pregnant. She had told him that day, before the hockey game. They had hugged until they had trouble breathing, and he would have stayed, missed the hockey game, but she insisted he go, the same way she insisted he attend the dinner.

He was remembering that morning, the way Marley looked, trying to imagine how she would look in seven months — still damn good, he bet — and he didn't hear his name being called from the head table, had to be nudged by the soldier next to him, pulled out of his revelry.

"Marc, you gotta go up."

"What?"

"You're being promoted, buddy. Get up there."

And he walked uncertainly to the head table, where the private was waiting for him with a pair of sergeant's stripes. He stood there not knowing what to say, as everyone at the head table laughed. Then he took the stripes and waved them above his head, applause echoing throughout the hangar; guys from his company standing up and clapping, their hands stretched over their heads.

Sergeant Léger. It was going to be a good Christmas.

* * *

Coalition Forces Land Component Command, Camp Doha, Kuwait

Major Jim McKillip stood in the doorway of Lieutenant-General Mikolashek's office, holding the papers that had been couriered to him from Ottawa. It was two days before Christmas. The American general looked up from his desk at the Canadian liaison officer and waved him inside.

"So what's this idea you have?" he said.

"Is it true you're looking for someone to go into Kandahar with the 101st?" said McKillip.

"It's a coalition. It would be nice to have someone go over there with them."

Mikolashek was commander of U.S. Army Forces Central Command, a thirty-two-year army veteran who had taken a liking to the young Canadian liaison officer.

"I know where there's a battle group ready to go," said McKillip, placing the binder down on the desk.

The general reached across to grab it. "Any good?"

"I think you'll like them"

PART II
Afghanistan

The line, broken into moving fragments by the ground, went calmly on through fields and woods. The youth looked at the men nearest him, and saw, for the most part, expressions of deep interest, as if they were investigating something that had fascinated them. One or two stepped with over valiant airs as if they were already plunged into war. Others walked as upon thin ice. The greater part of the untested men appeared quiet and absorbed. They were going to look at war, the red animal — war, the blood-swollen god. And they were deeply engrossed in this march.

— Stephen Crane, *The Red Badge of Courage*

How are you? You have been in Afghanistan, I perceive.

— Sir Arthur Conan Doyle, *A Study in Scarlet*

The car made its way from the Halifax airport, travelling down Highway 102 through Fall River and Waverley, past Bedford Basin. It was a hot August day and from the backseat, as they passed the basin, Pat Stogran thought he could see the bridge connecting Halifax to Dartmouth, although there was heat shimmering in the distance and he couldn't be certain.

He took the briefing booklet from his briefcase, reading the title one more time — Co & Rsm Visit Information Package — but put it on his lap and did not open it.

Bedford Basin: settled in 1751 by a ranger from New York named John Gorham, hired by the British to build a fort on the northwest shore. Gorham had built Fort Sackville good and strong, so that it never fell to the Mi'kmaq or the Acadians or the man who led them, Father Jean-Louis Le Loutre, even though Halifax itself was raided many times. Father Le Loutre's War, as it was called, lasted six years.

Father Le Loutre, not being able to match the British in numbers or firepower, fought a war of ambushes, raids, and quick-hit skirmishes. A petite guerre, he called it. Stogran looked at Bedford Basin, heat waves shimmering over the water so you lost the horizon after a while and the basin looked as though you were beneath the water itself, staring up, the surface no longer defined, everything opaque and distorted. A Jesuit priest fighting a petite guerre. Two weeks out of Afghanistan, he wasn't sure what to make of that.

He flipped open the booklet and started reading:

Itinerary
CO/RSM visit to Nova Scotia and Ontario
1 August–4 August
Concept

1) Almost immediately upon the arrival of the 3 PPCLI BG from South West Asia, the Commanding Officer LCol Stogran and the Regimental Sergeant-Major CWO Comeau, in addition to the RSM's wife, will conduct a personal visit of the gravesites of Sergeant Léger, Cpl Dyer and Ptes Smith and Green. It is their

intention to pay their final respects at the resting places of the four fallen soldiers. Where possible and time permitting, the CO and RSM will visit families in the immediate area.

Stogran found himself wishing the soldier who put the briefing booklet together had used a different word for the next section, but it was a military word, and after thinking about it for a minute he had to admit he couldn't come up with a better word than "execution." He kept reading.

2) The entire trip will take place over four days. The party will initially fly to Halifax and then work their way west.

   a. On Day One they will be greeted at the Halifax airport by an Escorting Officer. He will drive them to Hubbards were they will view Pte. Green's grave and visit with the Green family. Pte Smith's ashes were spread at Peggy's Cove, which will be visited next, prior to the overnight stop in Truro. A handover of Escorting Officers will take place at this point in Truro.

   b. Day Two sees the party visiting the Smith family home in Tatamagouche, where the father has erected a small memorial in his son's honour. The party will then be taken back to the Halifax airport for the evening flight to Ottawa. They will be met at the McDonald-Cartier Airport by an Escorting Officer. He will drive them immediately to Cornwall for an overnight stay.

   c. On the third day, the CO and RSM will visit Sergeant Léger's gravesite in nearby

Lancaster, ON, and spend some time with
the Léger parents. After lunch, the party will
be driven to Toronto for a rendezvous with
the succeeding Escort Officer. They will view
Cpl Dyer's gravesite that evening and visit the
Dyer father. The CO and RSM will stay overnight in Toronto and leave the next morning,
arriving in Edmonton at lunch time.

He closed the booklet and put it on the seat next to him. He barely
remembered Ricky Green. That was the truth of it. The thing he didn't
want to admit, but couldn't lie about either. Green had been a young
kid, twenty-one years old when A Company went to that training range.
Stogran had looked at Green's service photos, studied the face, tried to
remember when they may have crossed paths, but nothing other than
vague, face-in-the-crowd images ever came to him.

The briefing notes told him Green had been raised in Hubbards, Nova
Scotia, parents separated, an only child raised by his mother. He'd graduated from Forest Heights Community School in June 1998, enlisted the
following September. One last summer blowout in Nova Scotia, it looked
like. He'd completed Battle School and been posted to the 3rd Battalion in
May 1999, then transferred to A Company even though he hadn't finished
all his jump courses. Someone, somewhere, must have thought the kid
was going to do all right.

Stogran just couldn't remember him.

The car drove not to the mother's house, but to that of Petty Officer
Herb McDonald (retired). Stogran had read about him in the newspaper
stories attached to the briefing booklet, a family friend who had spoken
at Green's funeral. He was called a mentor, a man who had a lot of influence on Green; probably had something to do with the kid enlisting. The
RSM knocked on the door and the petty officer answered. The mother's
name was Doreen Young, and she was inside waiting. Later that day they
would drive by her house, a mobile trailer where she had raised her son.
Stogran guessed that's why they had gone to the petty officer's house, she

didn't want them inside her trailer, not that he would have cared. He'd grown up with plenty of kids who'd lived in mobile homes. Just meant you didn't have a lot of money. That was all.

The mother had made sandwiches and coffee. Stogran sat across a dining-room table from her, while the RSM and the retired petty officer sat in couches. She was a slight woman, with blonde hair cut soldier length, glasses, her forearms lean and with definition, Stogran not surprised to learn she had spent her life working on the line at a canning factory, then for some local janitorial companies after the canning factory closed.

He had rehearsed what he wanted to say, and after he had accepted a sandwich, a coffee, asked her questions about life in Hubbards, he said it: "I'm sorry we didn't bring Ricky home."

Young didn't say anything, so he continued. "That was my job, bringing him home, and I didn't. I'll never forgive myself for that. He was a —" and here he hesitated, not sure what he could say about a man he didn't know, then deciding it was safe to say what the briefing booklet had told him "— good soldier. He was doing well."

"He was so proud," said Young. "He loved being a parachutist. He would have stayed a long time."

"I know."

"It's not fair."

"It isn't."

Private Richard Green.

They both fell silent, then were surprised when, a few seconds later, they heard sobs. They turned their heads and saw the RSM and the petty officer — two giant men — hugging each other on the couch. The RSM had known Green well. Not knowing what to do, Stogran averted his eyes and stared at his shoes.

After leaving McDonald's house they drove to a provincial Manpower office, where in the back of the building a small lane had been named Pte. Richard Green Lane. Next to the building a sugar maple had also been planted in Green's honour. There was no plaque for the tree, but Young said one was being made and would be there before Christmas.

They stood by the tree without a plaque, people walking in and out of the Manpower office and pointing to them. Looking at the steady stream of people, Stogran found it no surprise Green had come from a place like Hubbards. Sometimes he'd look at a nominal roll and the places where soldiers came from, he didn't recognize most of them. Inlet-this, Bay-that, rural kids coming from places where the work had disappeared a long time ago. They tended to make good soldiers. If there were still decent jobs for working-class kids, the army recruiters would have a tougher job, and the army wouldn't be nearly as good.

When they had finished standing in front of the tree they made their way back to the cars. Young had not asked him a lot of questions about her son, and Stogran was grateful. Perhaps she had guessed he wouldn't know Ricky all that well. Didn't want to embarrass him. She had asked him more questions about Afghanistan, what it had been like there; the living conditions; Operation Anaconda, which he gathered the local paper had covered in detail, the first combat mission since the Korean War, a Hubbards boy in the thick of it.

He had answered as best he could, although he was surprised when he'd stumbled a few times. Perhaps he didn't want her to know every-thing — the living conditions were primitive, to be kind — but then he wondered if it might have been something else. Maybe he didn't know the answers? Maybe he hadn't made up his mind about Afghanistan?

They drove down the gravel road, a light breeze coming in off St. Margaret's Bay, Stogran remembering the past six months.

CHAPTER NINE

The request went from Kuwait to Coalition Central Command in Tampa Bay, Florida, on to National Defence Headquarters in Ottawa, then across the desks of Ray Henault and Art Eggleton, until finally reaching Prime Minister Jean Chrétien.

The Americans were deploying the 101st Airborne Division to the Kandahar Airfield, to relieve the United States 26th Marine Expeditionary Unit, which had seized the airport from Taliban forces in early December. The request from Coalition Central Command was for Canadian ground troops to deploy alongside the Americans. Nearly three months after Operation Enduring Freedom had begun, the Americans were finally requesting Canadian soldiers to help in the war in Afghanistan.

The American request had everything the Canadian government was looking for. It was not for "bits and pieces" of the 3rd Battalion Battle Group. The Americans were requesting the entire battle group — the light infantry soldiers, engineers, medics, Lord Strathcona's Horsemen, and their Coyote Reconnaissance Vehicles.

The Americans also needed a quick answer. The 101st were going to start relieving the Marines in two weeks.

Pat Stogran was out running, listening to AC/DC on the portable CD player his wife had given him for Christmas — "Hell's Bells," and how could you do a pace-yourself jog when you're listening to that song? Full-bore run. Turning the song up louder when his cellphone started vibrating.

He fumbled for the button to pause the CD, then flipped open his phone. It was Steve Borland, at the Edmonton Garrison.

"We just got a warning order you need to see."

"Now?"

"I would say now. Yes, definitely now."

* * *

Stogran had another read through the warning order, just to make sure he wasn't imagining the words in front of him. He had returned from Northwood less than two weeks ago, perhaps the most embarrassing trip in his military career, stuck wearing camos in a roomful of parade generals, sent home after a wasted week, detained at the Ottawa airport by a customs official who kept asking him why a Canadian army officer would need a C-7 rifle, because "all you guys do are peacekeeping missions," like they were all using water balloons in Bosnia.

Stogran had begun to suspect there would be no ground component to Operation Apollo, combat or any other deployment. The whole thing was starting to look like an incredible muddle back in Ottawa. And now here he was, looking at a warning order that said there was going to be a press conference the following morning at National Defence Headquarters, and if he could get his troops to the garrison before the conference started he could tell them personally that they were being deployed to Afghanistan.

There were no other details. Just that tasking orders were forthcoming.

The tasking orders came late that night, arriving as a flash message, so they were driven immediately to Stogran's home. The package was the size of a two-volume Oxford Dictionary. Stogran was almost overwhelmed looking at it, although it had a good index, and when he ran his finger down the page he found what he was looking for. He flipped to the section on rules of engagement.

Five minutes later he closed the book, stood up, and looked at his wife, who was standing nearby.

"Well?" she asked.

Stogran didn't answer right away.

Marc Léger left his house at 6:30 the next morning. The CO wanted every-one in the hangar by 0:800 and it was going to be some serious announce-ment. Soldiers had been called off leave. People still on Christmas holiday were told to wrap it up, get their ass back to the garrison.

"Looks like we got our orders," he'd said when he came through the door the previous night, although to his wife's repeated questioning he said he didn't know much more than that. Big announcement. Everyone in the hangar. CO going to address the troops. That's about it.

"So why do you think it's about the deployment?" she'd asked. "Couldn't it be something else?"

"Could be anything," he'd agreed, "although it's the battle group that's been called in, not just the battalion. So it must have something to do with deploying."

That night they had a quiet dinner, even though a lot of A Company was already out celebrating, convinced they were on their way to Afghanistan. It was January 6th and some of the guys were looking for one last holiday blast, the as-yet-to-be-announced mission was as good an excuse as any. Marley was already getting tired in the evening so Marc took a pass. Besides, he had little interest in waking up with a hangover.

That was certainly different from how things used to be. When Marc was posted to Calgary with the 2nd Battalion of the Princess Patricia's Canadian Light Infantry, right after infantry training in Wainwright, Alberta, he used to practically live on Electric Avenue. Out every weekend. Going from bar to bar. Because of his size he was often getting tasked to settle disputes or back up a buddy who got into a jam. And the next morning, when they were out on PT? — nothing to it. He and his friends even had a theory that PT was the best way to cure a hangover.

Back in Cornwall, Marley graduated from high school and enrolled in the business administration program at St. Lawrence College. She wrote to Marc every week, although his return letters were less frequent. For three years they saw each other only on holidays and vacations. Marley was frustrated, and finally asked him, on a visit to Calgary, what he wanted to do. They couldn't go on like this forever.

"What do you want to do?" asked Marc.

"Be with you."

"Then maybe you should move out here."

So in 1995 she'd moved to Calgary and they took a small apartment. She was there only a month before Marc was posted to Edmonton to become part of the new parachute company. Almost as soon as she arrived in Edmonton, Marc was sent to Bosnia for a six-month peacekeeping mission. Marley sat in their apartment in Edmonton — where she had no job, no family, and no friends — and thought: "I'll give this a year."

That deployment to Bosnia changed him — seeing the way some people in the world had to live. When he returned he was less interested in going out with friends on a Saturday night. Less interested in doing PT with a hangover.

That Christmas, he'd proposed. He waited until Marley had opened her presents, then he went down on one knee and pulled a ring box from the pocket of his housecoat, the way he figured it should be done. Marley didn't even bother saying yes. She just hugged him until they fell on the floor.

Now they were expecting their first child — no doubt there would be more — and celebrating a deployment that was going to take him away from her for God knows how long, why would he do a thing like that?

They watched television and went to bed early, Marc pulling his wife into his body, resting his arm on her belly, moving it around until she said: "You're not going to feel anything yet."

He pulled his hand away, feeling stupid.

Marc and Marley Léger on their wedding day.

* * *

Steve Borland had never seen his CO so jacked. The man couldn't sit down, couldn't stand still, just kept pacing the room, big long strides like he was out on parade, but with walls that kept forcing him to turn sooner than he wanted.

"The troops are at the hangar?"

"Yes, sir."

"The entire battle group?"

"Yes, sir."

"What time is it?"

"0:7:50"

"All right, let's go."

Stogran walked to the dais that had been set up at one end of the hangar. There was a microphone, but he wasn't going to need it.

"We have our orders," he said, and the troops gave a short round of applause. "I know a lot of you were expecting to deploy to Kabul. I was expecting that myself. Well, those are not our orders."

He waited a minute for that to sink in. At the regimental Christmas party he had even said — the last announcement he'd made from the head table — "I'll see you in Kabul." Stogran watched confused expressions spread across the faces of soldiers lined up directly in front of him. Some of them were probably wondering if they were still going to Afghanistan. Maybe the battalion was on its way back to Bosnia, to relieve some American troops there. Maybe Operation Apollo was going to pass them by completely. He waited until there was a murmur in the room, then said: "Our orders are to deploy to the Kandahar Airfield, chalks starting end of the month. We will be attached to the American 101st Airborne Division."

The murmurs turned to gasps. The 101st was about as storied a military unit as there was. The "Screaming Eagles" who'd landed on Utah Beach the night before D-Day; who helped win the war for the Allies during the Battle of The Bulge, when they refused to surrender to German forces while under siege in Bastogne. To the jumpers in A Company, this was like being told you were going on tour with the Rolling Stones.

"Once in Kandahar, our duties will be security around the Kandahar airport, exploration of sites already taken from Taliban government forces, prisoner supervision, and support for humanitarian assistance," continued Stogran. He gave another pause and then added: "We will also be tasked to eliminate Taliban and al Qaeda threats in the region."

It took a second to understand. Stogran had just told the troops they were going on a combat mission. The applause in the hangar started slowly, but within a minute it was as loud as a Hercules coming in for landing.

CHAPTER TEN

Later that week Stogran and an advance party of more than twenty soldiers flew out of Edmonton on their way to Kandahar, stopping in Ottawa en route for last minute briefings at NDHQ. In Ottawa they were told the Americans ran Kandahar and would have operational control, but Stogran had the final say on how to deploy his troops. It wouldn't be an easy thing to do, but he could say no if he needed to. Some opposition politicians and newspaper columnists were already criticizing the government for committing Canadian troops to an American-led combat mission. The name that had been given to the combined force was Task Force Rakkasan, the nickname for the 187th Infantry Regiment, the airborne soldiers who were already in Kandahar at battalion strength. Rakkasan is Japanese for falling umbrellas. The man who would be running Task Force Rakkasan was U.S. Colonel Frank Wiercinski.

The advance party flew into Kandahar in the middle of the night, the C-17 conducting a tactical landing — a series of evasive banks and dives — before landing. The Taliban had been chased out of this airfield only a month before, and every plane was making tactical landings. Once on the tarmac the Canadians waited several minutes for the back cargo door of the plane to open, rucksacks on their backs, C-7 rifles on their knees. They had been briefed to expect anything when they landed. Spread out. Return fire. Anything. What greeted them when the doors opened, however, was an airfield as busy as a commercial airport, headlights zigzagging through the night, shouted orders, the mechanized rumble of cargo trucks, forklifts, Jeeps. An American escort officer was there to take them to the terminal.

The advance team had a quick briefing on the military situation in Kandahar Province, the layout of the airfield, basic hygiene — what they could eat and drink, where they could defecate. Then the escort officer took then to the transient bivouac area, showed the Canadians their assigned tents, and left. The rucksacks were shoved under cots, the C-7s cached next to the rucksacks, and the Canadians tried to get some sleep. The night was surprisingly cold so some fished out their thermal sleeping bags, but after a few hours of fitful rest they gave up and went to explore the airfield.

* * *

Canadian troops in front of the terminal at Kandahar Airfield.

Back at the Edmonton Garrison the rest of the battle group was scrambling. The soldiers had just been told they had three weeks to pack up and deploy on Canada's first combat mission in forty-nine years. While the 3rd Battalion had deployed often to Bosnia and Croatia in the past decade, these had been peacekeeping missions and there had always been some sort of infrastructure. Command posts, watchtowers, mess halls, sleeping quarters had all been waiting for them. In Afghanistan there would be nothing. This was start-from-scratch-and-hope-you-don't-forget-anything time, or as the old hunting maxim goes: "You can survive just about anything in the bush except the stupidity that made you leave something important back in the truck."

Wayne Green started double-checking the pallets, making sure everything was there. The pallets were going to go into shipping containers, then onto cargo planes. Green didn't know what, exactly, they would be using for planes, but there better be a lot of them, or they better be big. He was going to have more than a hundred shipping containers by the time he was finished.

Glen Zilkalns moved a cot into his office while he tried to complete the JEMMS spreadsheets. He also put together a list of all the vehicles lined up on the tarmac. The transport pool had to inspect the vehicles, making sure they worked and had all the necessary fluids — even though he was sure many of them would be left on the tarmac when the battle group left Edmonton.

Each soldier had personal business to take care of as well. Insurance policies had to be checked and updated. Bills organized and paid. If joint accounts weren't already set up with their spouses and partners that had to be done, with arrangements made to have their pay deposited directly into the account. There were always some soldiers who never got around to organizing this, and on this deployment the commanding officers didn't want to be bothered with phone calls from the rear party, telling them a family was about be evicted because some soldier in their platoon forgot to open a joint bank account. Can you get them to sign the damn paperwork?

Sergeant Mark Pennie also had a lot of work to do in three weeks. The engineer was in charge of the battle group's reverse osmosis machine, a water purifier that needed to be one of the first pieces of equipment shipped to Kandahar. Sothern Afghanistan had been under a drought for years, and in their briefings the Canadians had been told potable water would be like gold during this deployment.

The seventeen-year military veteran took great pride in his water machine. It cost $1 million, had been used many times in the Balkans, and whenever a soldier got a bad case of diarrhea on an overseas mission and blamed it on the water, Pennie took it personally, tracking down the soldier and saying it wasn't the water. He would explain how the machine worked, that it filtered out everything except pure water molecules, which are smaller than most things in nature, so the water the soldier was drinking was 96.6 percent pure, my friend.

Pennie handled the crating of the machine himself, making sure every piece was properly wrapped and protected. He'd heard of the tactical landings into the Kandahar Airfield. He'd be up a creek — a badly contaminated creek — if his machine was damaged during transport.

In late January the soldiers being deployed to Afghanistan started getting briefings from Major Rod Keller, an engineer who had been part of the advance party into Kandahar. Keller had been in Afghanistan for three days and returned to the garrison to warn the soldiers about many things, starting with the mosquitoes.

Afghanistan is arid — as dry as bleached bones — yet somehow overrun with mosquitoes. For Canadians, who naturally associate mosquitoes with marshland and still water, this was going to take some getting used to. He warned them to take the malaria pills they would be given when they deployed.

Next Keller warned them about the sand, which would be flying around with the mosquitoes; sand everywhere, not just on bad days when there was a storm, but every day. It would get into their food, their tents, and, most importantly, their guns. They should try to keep that from happening. Number three on the hit-list of things to be careful about in Afghanistan: landmines. Perhaps even more prevalent than sand or mosquitoes. A few days before Keller had arrived in Kandahar, an Australian soldier had stepped on one and had to be airlifted to an American military hospital in Germany. Be aware of where you are at all times, he warned them.

Later, the soldiers were briefed by a Canadian JTF2 soldier who had spent nearly a year in the mountains around Kandahar, fighting with the mujahedeen, when he had been seconded to an American special-forces unit. Don't take these people lightly, the soldier told them. Yes, Kandahar had fallen and was in coalition control, but it was the last city to fall to the Americans, was surrounded by mountains and supply routes into Pakistan, and you would not go wrong assuming the rebels were still around. The Taliban would be a tough adversary. Just ask a Russian infantry soldier.

* * *

Back in Ottawa there was also a mad scramble going on, although this was a political one. Eggleton and Henault were fending off criticism about deploying an infantry battle group to Afghanistan on such short notice. As soon as the announcement was made, NDP Leader Alexa McDonough said the Liberal government had just ceded Canadian sovereignty to the Americans, and was now little more than a fifty-first state. She would also complain when, later that month, it was revealed that Canadian JTF2 troops had been handing over Taliban and al Qaeda prisoners to the Americans. The federal opposition leader said this was a contravention of the Geneva Convention, and Canadian soldiers should stay home in Edmonton.

The criticism was not just coming from the left of the political spectrum. Conservative Elsie Wayne took the government to task over the camouflage uniforms the soldiers would be wearing in Kandahar. While the Americans had deployed with desert camouflage, the Canadians would be wearing green. The revelation embarrassed both Eggleton and Henault, who argued that green camouflage is actually better, as it is harder to see at night. While there was some truth to their argument, the green-camouflage issue was a hit with editorial cartoonists across the country.

Along with prisoner exchanges, camouflage uniforms, and Canadian sovereignty, the defence minister and CDS were also answering questions about how prepared the soldiers in Edmonton were to go into combat. In Afghanistan, Peter Dawe, the battle group's operations officer and part of the advance party, told reporters what seemed obvious to him — there was a lot or work to do in three weeks. The battle group might not be fully operational until mid-February. This seemingly innocuous comment set off a political firestorm back in Ottawa, where opposition politicians and military analysts were quick to say the admission was proof that the Canadian Forces were being spread too thin. While a spokesperson for the Canadian Forces denied there would be a delay, Art Eggleton's office admitted it was possible.

Critics also start asking questions about how the battle group would even get to Afghanistan, as the Canadian Forces had no planes capable of doing the job. The lack of airlift capability was something highlighted in

Auditor General Sheila Fraser's annual report to Parliament the previous month, a document that painted a bleak picture of a Canadian military with aging equipment, dwindling troops, and low morale.

Shortly before the troops deployed to Kandahar, Henault answered the critics by giving a lengthy interview to the *Toronto Star*, telling the newspaper that sending a battle group to Afghanistan was indeed an ambitious plan, one that would tax the capabilities of the Canadian Forces, but would succeed.

"Given the commitment that we've just undertaken, to deploy our infantry battle group to Afghanistan, it would be difficult to take on another major mission at this stage of the game," Henault admits. "It's a very high operational tempo. I would say that we've actually surged to the degree that is possible. We're doing all that we can at the moment, but we now have to balance that off so we can sustain it in the longer term."

The Americans ended up sending the planes. C-5 Galaxys started to arrive in Edmonton during the last week of January. The C-5s are the largest cargo planes in the United States military and most of them are booked two years in advance — the rotation of American troops and equipment being a logistical puzzle that keeps an entire department in the Pentagon gainfully employed year after year. Zilkalns, the soldier in the battle group with a better under-standing of logistical requirements than anyone else, was impressed.

The first thing the Americans did was ask Zilkalns what in hell a JEMMS spreadsheet is. They needed everything in Excel.

After that they start loading equipment onto the planes: storage containers, Coyotes, the reverse osmosis water purification system, the Iltis Jeeps and trucks — both LSVWs and MLVWs — a BV-206 as well, a multi-track, all-terrain vehicle that is good in snow. While more vehicles went on the planes than Zilkalns had thought, scores of them were left parked on the tarmac when the last of the battle group left Edmonton. He wondered who would come and pick them up.

The Americans-to-the-rescue plan quickly hit a snag though, which more than a few Canadian soldiers secretly enjoyed, embarrassed as they were by being airlifted into combat by another country. The American planes started breaking down.

Master-Corporal Danielle Bernier, Combat Camera

As a part of their daily routine, two Medium Logistics Vehicles, Wheeled (MLVW) from the Lord Strathcona's Horse (LdSH) (RC) RECCE Squadron, one carrying fuel and the other carrying food and water, make their way around the perimeter of the Kandahar Airfield to resupply Coalition Observation Posts.

A C-5 breaking down is not like a car blowing a gasket. The parts are expensive and almost certainly not found anywhere close to Edmonton. The Americans had originally planned on sending two C-5s to move the Canadians. Then they had to dispatch another. And another. And another. In the end, five C-5s were dispatched to Edmonton to airlift the battle group to Afghanistan, a debacle that embarrassed the Americans and started to frustrate the Canadian soldiers.

On several occasions a Canadian platoon arrived for its chalk and, after a tearful goodbye to family in the hangar at the base, boarded the buses heading to the airport only to arrive at the airport and discover the plane had broken down. After sitting on their rucksacks for the rest of the day, they would re-board the buses and head back to the garrison. Many soldiers complained to Zilkalns about the delays, saying it was almost cruel, making their families go through multiple departures. Like there was something he could do about it. Like he was a part-time C-5 mechanic and just hadn't told anyone.

* * *

With his Christmas promotion to sergeant, Marc Léger found himself with a new job. He was working in the company storeroom, second-in-command to A Company Quartermaster Billy Bolen. It was Léger's job to make sure the company had all the kit and supplies it would need in Afghanistan, and because of this he was one of the last soldiers to leave Edmonton. It was the morning of February 9th when he left his home, a trim bungalow in northeast Edmonton, for the short drive to the base, Marley sitting next to him in the cab of the truck.

Along the way they talked of the upcoming mission. Léger once again assured Marley that the battalion would probably see limited, if any, action. It had taken months just to receive their orders to ship overseas, he reminded her, a typical muddle back in Ottawa. Plus, Canadians rarely saw combat, even in the world's hot spots. Get shipped to Bosnia and you man observation posts. Go to the Gulf War and you guard POWs. Afghanistan would be more of the same, even if it were considered a combat mission.

As Léger drove he continued talking. He loved to talk. He was usually in a good mood, the words tumbling out in a torrent when he felt particularly excited or nervous, which he was that morning. Marley knew not everything he was saying was true, but she didn't argue. She let him talk, knowing he was trying to reassure her, and that this was important to him.

Just a few weeks earlier, Marley had lost her baby. She was at fourteen weeks and one morning she started bleeding. Six hours later a doctor was telling her he was sorry. There was no specific cause. Don't try to figure it out or you'll go mad. These things happened sometimes.

It had been a sad time since and, had he chosen, Marc could have walked into Hackett's office and asked not to go to Afghanistan. He was needed at home. But he never considered it. He had to go. He had told Marley the night before that this might be the only chance he'd get to "truly do what I've been trained to do."

When they reached the garrison, Marc quickly went to work. He was a big man — six foot three, 230 pounds — and Marley enjoyed watching the way he moved. He had the grace of a long-distance runner, a natural gait many big men lack.

Shortly before 10:00 a.m., when all the weapons had been distributed and the paperwork completed, Marc walked her back to the truck. Saying goodbye would be unbearable. They had decided earlier that she would leave before the buses departed.

They stood in the parking lot and embraced quickly, the sun still hidden behind low clouds, the wind strong. "Come back safe," she said. "And don't you dare forget me."

"How could I forget you?" he laughed. "I'll phone as soon as I can. To see how you and Hunter are doing." Hunter was their new golden retriever. Léger was glad they had him. At least Marley would not be completely alone these next few months.

They embraced again and then she left. A short time later, Marc boarded the bus for the airport. He flew directly to a U.S. base near Frankfurt, then on to Kandahar.

CHAPTER ELEVEN

What most soldiers notice first about Afghanistan is a smell. Before their eyes ever see the mountains, or their ears hear the roars of military cargo planes, before any of the other senses kick in, they notice a smell.

Most of them later describe it as a "musty" smell, or a "stale" smell, the scent of a thing that had been boarded up and abandoned for a long time, then suddenly opened. It's at the other end of the olfactory spectrum from the bracing winds and winter pine — the new-world scents — of northern Alberta in February.

When they discussed it later among themselves, how best to describe the smell, some attempting to associate it with other scents, the comparison that seemed most apt was opening an old aunt's sock drawer stuffed with mothballs. Perhaps not quite as chemically.

The first Canadian soldiers arrived in Kandahar on February 2. There were twenty-five of them, landing on the Kandahar Airfield at 4:30 a.m. Pat Stogran was there to greet them as they got off the plane, then he escorted them to their briefings inside the terminal. The night was too black for any of the soldiers to get a good look at what surrounded them.

Three hours later another plane landed with forty-five Canadian soldiers and a Coyote. The sun had risen by then and the soldiers craned their necks as they were escorted to the terminal, looking at the bullet scars on the terminal building, the boarded-up windows, the still shadowy outline of a Soviet-era tank sitting in a field.

Inside the terminal they were given an orientation briefing by an American major, who didn't seem overly pumped to see them sitting in his terminal. A few days later they would learn a rifle company from the 187th had been left behind to make way for the Canadians, and it hadn't sat well with the rest of the soldiers in the American battalion. They probably would have felt the same way if it had been reversed, so they put up with the grumbling over the next few weeks as best they could.

The major showed on a topographical map where the enemy was thought to be hiding, where there had been some recent firefights, the layout of the camp itself, the security line the Marines were currently manning, which the Canadians would take over in less than two weeks, as soon as the rest of the battle group arrived. The RIPs — relief in place — were slated to begin in ten days.

When the briefing was finished, the sun had snuck completely over the mountains to the east and north. As they were escorted to the transient bivouac, the Canadians were surprised by how much activity was going on around them: forklifts scurrying around taking pallets and shipping containers off cargo planes; special forces personnel smoking by a chain-link fence, Berettas stuffed in the back of their spandex pants; a demining machine in the distance, working on the patch of ground that would soon be the Canadian camp, the steel-tendons of the machine lashing out like whips in the rising sun, pounding the ground and throwing up so much dust it reminded some of the soldiers of morning mist rising off a lake.

When they passed the plane they had just arrived on they heard a small cheer coming from the Americans unloading the cargo. A Coyote was backing its way down the ramp. Above its licence plate was a hand-written sign reading "I Love New York."

On February 11, five months after the terrorist attacks in the United States, three pipers gathered on the ground cleared by the demining machine. As the sun rose behind them, they played "The Maple Leaf Forever." The 334 Canadian troops that had arrived in Afghanistan stood and watched, as did several hundred American paratroopers.

As the pipers played, the Canadian flag was raised on a pole erected in the middle of the tents, trailers, and trucks that made up the Canadian base. When the flag was flying, Stogran announced the Canadian troops were "operational." After that, Colonel Wiercinski welcomed the Canadians to Taskforce Rakkasan. "I bless you all," he said. "As Shakespeare said, 'We few, we happy few, we band of brothers.'"

* * *

Canadian soldiers started relieving Marines on the line later that same day. The security perimeter stretched completely around the airfield, 1.5 kilometres wide by four kilometres long. On the other side of the line was a barbed-wire fence, separating the airfield from the rest of Afghanistan. The Americans did not patrol outside the wire, nor had any attempt been made to clear it of landmines, many of which were no doubt there, left over from the war with the Soviets.

The line was about as rudimentary as it gets. There were no watch-towers. No stationary surveillance outposts. The Marines had put up their surveillance equipment on eight-metre high piles of gravel, and dug two-man foxholes. Humvee Jeeps were concealed behind sandbags. The Canadians were used to security perimeters in Bosnia and Croatia that had been built by engineers, and had been there for years. This was like something out of an old war movie.

By February 13th all the Marines had been relieved and the Canadians had control of the line. Their surveillance equipment was the Coyotes, which had radar-like motion detectors called "M-Star," and an optical camera with night-vision capabilities. If the motion detectors picked up anything moving out in the no-man's land, an alarm would sound in the Coyotes and the camera would hone in on what the radar had detected. Stray dogs could trigger it, which became annoying before long.

Still, there weren't just stray dogs out there. Just about every day on the line the Canadians could track trucks moving outside the wire. The trucks would arrive with men atop the bed, who would jump off as the truck stopped, then disappear from sight. Whoever was out there, they had their own foxholes. One night two men were spotted near the fence, much closer than the trucks ever were. When an American patrol was dispatched, the men fled. Before fleeing, though, they had dug what looked like two mortar placements.

If the line was rudimentary, the airfield was primitive.

There were no latrines and no running water. The soldiers urinated in piss tubes and defecated in cut-down oil drums. The fifty-five-gallon drums were burned every afternoon, the stench wafting over the camp, a rancid choking smell that would stay until dawn. The heat didn't help matters, the mid-afternoon temperatures already twenty-five degrees Celsius, the nights bitterly cold. The soldiers slept in winter sleeping bags, then sweated inside their flak jackets when they awoke.

They ate MREs for every meal, three-squares of dehydrated food that tasted bad the first day and never got any better. Until Pennie's water-purification system was up and running, they were limited to three litres of water per day, which included washing and making the dehydrated meals. When they weren't on the line they slept in four-man tents that couldn't comfortably house four soldiers with full kit and weapons. Luckily, Green had shipped over plenty of tents and two soldiers eventually shared each one, with enough room to get cots wedged inside. It might have been the one luxurious touch of the entire deployment.

When they weren't manning the line, or sleeping in their tents, the soldiers familiarized themselves with the rest of the airfield. The terminal had been built by the United States Agency for International Development in the early sixties, as a military base in the event of a showdown with the U.S.S.R. At that time the U.S.S.R. had been building its own airport in Kabul. The airfield was occupied by the Soviets in 1979 and severely damaged in the ensuing war with the mujahedeen. It had been damaged again only weeks earlier, during fierce fighting between the Taliban and U.S. Marines.

The terminal was shattered, the sort of building that remind you of newsreels of London after the blitz, or European cities after the Allied liberation. It was surrounded by Soviet-era army barracks with walls blown away, roofs gaping, buildings so badly damaged the Americans had not even tried to use them, choosing to pitch tents instead.

Around the barracks were the burned-out shells of Soviet tanks, Jeeps, trucks. There was a former rose garden in front of the terminal, once one of the largest gardens in the country, now little more than scorched earth, although a tangle of thorny brambles remained. The soldiers were surprised to see the remains of the rose garden, and to learn that Kandahar had once been considered a paradise, the breadbasket of Afghanistan. After years of drought, and years more of war, it was the sort of story you heard and didn't believe. Like a child's fable, an old man's fishing story, although the liaison officers that were supposed to know these things insisted it was true.

While most of the Canadian soldiers stayed inside the wire perimeter of the airfield, Pat Stogran, Steve Borland, and some of the other senior Canadian officers were taken to nearby Kandahar city, where the dichotomy between past glories and present realities was even more pronounced. Kandahar, the officers were told on their "cultural briefings" to the city, is located in one of the oldest human settlement areas in the world. The remains of peasant farming villages going back to 5,000 B.C. had been excavated not far from the city. It was once part of the Persian Empire, conquered by Alexander the Great, then conquered and re-conquered by virtually every empire to rise in southern Asia over the next two millennia.

All of that history was on display, not hard to find, from the mausoleum of Ahmad Shah in the centre of the city (the man who founded an independent Afghanistan in the mid-1700s) to the Da Shahidanu Chowk, a monument to Islamic martyrs standing in the centre of Kandahar's main market square. In front of Ahmad Shah's mausoleum there was even one of the most valued relics in the Muslim world, the Shrine of the Cloak, containing a shawl said to be have been worn by the Prophet Muhammad.

The city has a population of about half a million people, most living a subsistence existence. The former economic base of the city has been shattered by war and drought. Bordered by the Arghandab River to the west, Kandahar was built on an alluvial cone. With proper irrigation the land is fertile. This region was once an oasis, with orchards and gardens, fields of cotton and wheat, and flocks of sheep and goats. As the Canadians were driven around the city they saw abandoned food-processing plants and textile factories, sad reminders of what had once been.

The reasons for the constant strife in the region were also explained to them. Kandahar was built on what is known as the Asian Highway, an ancient trade route connecting the Indian subcontinent with the Middle East, Central Asia, and the Persian Gulf. The army that controlled Kandahar controlled the trade route, and what should have brought prosperity to the region had brought nothing but war and chaos. The area reminded Borland of Poland and the Balkans, places in Europe where, because of geography and nothing more, people had been consigned to centuries of hardship and calamity. Kandahar made a mockery of human endeavour.

If life in the city was grim, it was worse in the nearby villages. Because of the once-fertile land, Kandahar Province has one of the largest rural populations in Afghanistan. There are scores of villages on the plains that run up to the Pakistan border, and dotting the banks of the Arghandab and Tarnak rivers. Many of the villages no longer have flocks of sheep and goats to tend, or fields to till.

Despite the many hardships, despite the drought and the constant swirl of war, the Canadians heard few complaints from the people they met outside the airfield. On one visit to the city, Borland was told the story of Ahmad Shah, who in 1747 marched his army not far from Kandahar. Overnight the temperature had plummeted and the Afghan commander lost 18,000 soldiers. The next day he continued his march. Later that year he founded a country. As a Canadian boy from Peterborough, Borland knew about volatile weather. He respected a story like that. How could you not?

CHAPTER TWELVE

It's hard to keep a good peacekeeper down. Within days of taking over the line from American Marines, Canadian soldiers started visiting nearby villages. This had been standard Canadian military procedure all the way back to Cyprus. Canadians do not just man security perimeters, or keep warring sides at a safe distance, when deployed on peacekeeping missions. They go out on recce patrols — meet the people living where they are deployed to find out what would make their lives easier, and often try to make that happen.

This isn't a completely altruistic exercise. Winning the hearts and minds of the locals had been a military principle since the days of Sun Tzu, a way of protecting your army from insurgents and spies, sneak attacks and ambushes. But if others had seen the wisdom of such a tactic, Canadian soldiers had come close to perfecting it.

Combat Camera

Captain Alex Watson handing out school supplies.

Within days of arriving at the Kandahar Airfield, Stogran sent out a recce patrol. The man he had handpicked to be his civilian-military co-operation officer in Afghanistan, Captain Alex Watson, had done similar work in Bosnia. Stogran had been impressed with the young captain, even though he'd had to sneak Watson into Afghanistan. When the nominal roll was being drafted for the battle group, it didn't include a civilian-military co-operation officer. The generals in charge of the mission didn't see the need for one on a non-peacekeeping mission. When Stogran formally requested one, NDHQ turned him down. He added Watson's name anyway, assigning him to the recce platoon, and as soon as Watson had unpacked his kit Stogran told the captain to get to work.

Nothing Watson had seen in the Balkans prepared him for Afghanistan. He would arrive in villages that contained no adults, because everyone was out working in the fields. The children would descend on the Canadians like locust, ripping candy bars out of their hands and scampering over their vehicles, as though the Canadians had just walked into the pages of *Lord of the Flies*. The village wells had dried up, or were of such poor quality that they registered as sewage when Watson took water back to the airfield for Pennie to test. Every building in every village seemed to have been shelled

Canadian medic Sandi McIntyre, during a visit to Ahabudullah Kali village.

Master-Corporal Danielle Bernier, Combat Camera

and never repaired. Every village had tracts of land that had been mined, a no-man's land the villagers could not repair and had long ago learned to accept and avoid.

After these initial reports, Stogran started sending out engineers and medics to accompany Watson. The engineers began inspecting buildings, to see if any could be turned into schools. Medics started giving inoculation shots to the children, examining their parents, leaving behind bandages and disinfectants. When the engineers reported back that several of the villages had buildings that could easily be converted into schools, Stogran put in a request to the Canadian International Development Agency (CIDA) for money. It took weeks for the development agency to respond, and in that time Stogran read a news story, written by a journalist who had heard about the request for money to build Afghan schools. In the story, a CIDA spokesperson was quoted as saying: "We're looking at their request. All of this has to go through various procedures. We don't consider that as being held up and neither does national defence."

Stogran put down the newspaper, thinking if any schools were going to be built the soldiers would be doing it.

That's what happened. In the spring and early summer of 2002, nearly a dozen villages around Kandahar had schools built by Canadian engineers, who scrounged the building materials from the airfield, dismantling Soviet military barracks, bartering with the Americans for paint and mortar. While they built the schools the engineers also repaired the wells, and fixed some homes.

The tribal councils in the villages said they had teachers, which left only one thing lacking before the schools could be used — books, paper, and pencils. Stogran briefly considered putting in another request to CIDA but figured the soldiers would be back in Edmonton before the request made it through the "various procedures." Besides, the Canadians had been in this situation before, when they'd built schools in the Balkans, and they knew what the next step should be. They needed to get their families involved.

Wives and husbands at the Edmonton Garrison and CFB Shilo, where a company of infantry soldiers from the Patricia's 2nd Battalion had been attached to the battle group, started opening letters that, as well as the normal griping about weather and shitcans, had requests for school supplies. Could they send something over in the next package? Looking for books, pencils, pens, and anything else that came to mind. By April, Colonel Wiercinski was forced to go to the Canadian command post and complain to Stogran that so many school supplies were being shipped into the Kandahar Airfield that the mail system was breaking down.

"I'm told we're getting sea containers worth of books," said the American colonel. "We just can't handle it."

It was Watson who came up with the solution to that problem. Instead of sending school supplies, maybe people back in Canada could send money? Maybe a registered charity of some sort could be set up? Once again, CIDA and the Department of National Defence said they would consider the request, and once again the soldiers decided not to wait. A bank account was opened in Edmonton, where families could make donations. A lawyer started the paperwork to register as a charity.

Once the money started flowing, Stogran made arrangements with the Americans to use their cargo planes for shopping trips to Dubai. He had previously made arrangements to use the planes for four-day R&R visits to Dubai, a mid-mission break for the troops. Early in the deployment he'd noticed that the regularly scheduled flights were never at capacity, there was always room for a few soldiers to squeeze on. What would be the harm, he asked the Americans, if the soldiers started coming back with a few shopping bags?

The plan worked perfectly. Every R&R trip to Dubai had a soldier tasked with buying school supplies for Watson. The soldiers started fighting over who would get the job. There was so much money in the bank account — families at military bases across Canada had started fundraising drives — the soldiers could buy more than just school supplies. Chocolate bars, stuffed animals, comic books, clothing — it was all bought in Dubai, shipped back to Kandahar, and then stored in Wayne Green's regimental storeroom until Watson could distribute it.

Years later, when Canadian soldiers returned to Kandahar, many of the villagers around the airfield had only one question for the troops, once they spotted the Maple Leaf on the recce vehicles: "Where is Captain Watson?" they asked.

Master-Corporal Danielle Bernier, Combat Camera

Bombardier Dale Boyd helps distribute shoes in the village of Ahabudullah Kali.

CHAPTER THIRTEEN

The Shah-e-Kot Valley is the gateway to the Takur Ghar and Pecawul Ghar mountains, in eastern Afghanistan. Since Operation Enduring Freedom had begun, the mountains had been used by thousands of al Qaeda and Taliban fighters fleeing to Pakistan.

It wasn't long before the fighters returned. They came back down the mountain paths leading into Pakistan and entered the villages in the valley. They told the villagers that they had returned to fight the Americans.

More fighters had returned than had fled. Some of the new men were from Chechnya, or Uzbekistan; tough looking men who said little. The fighters said the villagers could join them or they could leave. The villagers left and the fighters took over their homes, moved into caves in the mountains, and waited.

Operation Anaconda, an American-led assault on the Shah-e-Kot Valley, began on March 2, 2002. It was the first large-scale battle in Afghanistan since the Battle of Tora Bora the previous December, and the Americans had spent two months planning it. Intelligence reports said high-value targets (HVTs) such as Jalaluddin Haqqani, the Taliban militant credited with introducing suicide bombing to the Afghan war, might be hiding in the valley.

The military planners devised a plan similar to Tora Bora. Fire support was to come from the United States Air Force, augmented by United States Navy units and the French Air Force. After the air assault, Colonel Wiercinski's 3rd Battalion would move into the valley. The American 10th Mountain Division would deploy to the mountains, to act as a "blocker" and round up any rebels running from the American soldiers.

The military planners estimated the rebel strength at around two hundred, and assumed the battle would unfold much like Tora Bora, where the rebels fled from the air assault. The planners ended up being wrong on both fronts. The rebel strength was later estimated at closer to a thousand. And they did not run.

When Operation Anaconda began, Pat Stogran was contacted by Colonel Wiercinski and told Canadian soldiers were needed to augment American forces fighting in the Shah-e-Kot Valley. The head of Task Force Rakkasan wanted Canadians to deploy in the mountains surrounding the valley, under command of the 10th Mountain Division. They would be sent to Tergul Ghar, a 3,500-metre-high mountain that is seven kilometres long and three kilometres wide, called the Whale's Back (or just the Whale) because of its irregular shape and many protruding ridges and cliffs.

The Whale had played a large role in thwarting the American assault when it began on March 2. Scores of rebels were dug into the mountain-side, firing mortars and rocket-propelled grenades onto the American soldiers. They fought from bunkers, caves, and other heavily fortified positions. Rather than being a place where the Americans thought they would round up fleeing rebels, the Whale was a highly effective rebel line. In keeping with the name of the mountain, the Canadian mission was given the code name Operation Harpoon.

On March 13th Canadian soldiers were airlifted to an airfield in Bagram, then loaded onto Black Hawk helicopters for the fifty-five-minute flight to the Whale. They disembarked halfway up the mountain. Their orders were to locate any bunkers or fortified positions that had survived a week-long air assault by American and French jets. If they found any rebels, they were to be captured or killed.

It was the first time since the Korean War that Canadian soldiers had been deployed with such orders.

The Canadians would stay on the Whale for four days, a logistical night-mare for Wayne Green, who was tasked with making sure the soldiers were supplied throughout the mission. Among the many firsts for Operation Harpoon was the fact it was totally air supported. In every peacekeeping mission of the past five decades, there had been roads to move soldiers and their supplies. On the Whale there were no highways, no roads, not even a path that a vehicle could travel down. All of the supplies for the Canadian soldiers had to be airlifted into them, from the fifteen litres of water each soldier consumed per day to the MREs and bullets.

Members of 3rd Battalion shortly before boarding a Chinook helicopter during Operation Harpoon.

There had never been a drill for this sort of deployment, never been a training exercise. Green had less than a week to come up with a plan that would get the Canadian supplies from Kandahar to the airfield at Bagram, then onto the Whale, a 300-kilometre supply line that would be totally dependent on American air support. It's one of those things you don't think about unless you're actually there, unless you're a soldier about to be deployed. While press releases were being sent from NDHQ, telling the country that Canadian soldiers were going on their first combat mission in forty-nine years, the soldiers themselves were left trying to figure out how to make that work. Where could they get a helicopter? Did they have enough water? It was not all that different from the weeks after Kabul fell, when Canadians were reading that soldiers could be deployed to Afghanistan within days, while the soldiers themselves were buying toilet paper and bottled water at a Shoppers Drug Mart in Edmonton.

Somewhat surprisingly, the airlift worked. The Canadians stayed in the field for four days and never had a problem being resupplied. Over the next ten years in Afghanistan, an airlift supply line became a well-oiled operational machine. A new skill for Canadian soldiers.

All three infantry companies of the battle group went on Op Harpoon, along with a platoon of mortars, a direct-fire support unit, an administrative company, and a squadron of engineers. Six snipers from the battalion had been seconded to the American Special Forces and had gone up earlier, as part of Operation Anaconda.

It was arduous going. Much of the Whale is covered in shale and the Canadians seemed to slip a step for every two they took. There are switch-back paths to follow up the side of the mountain, but often the paths had been blown away by the air assault, or were blocked by fallen rocks, so the recce patrols leading the way had to make sweeping detours, or find their own path up the mountain, drawing a bead on a ridgeline, reaching it, then start climbing toward the next.

They hadn't gone far before they starting finding remnants of rebel camps. Most were in caves, or close to caves, and every time one was found the soldiers had to determine if anyone was left hiding then call in the engineers, who would destroy them. That first night most of the soldiers slept on ridgelines, without tents, taking turns keeping watch under a starry sky, the valley below lighting up with bombs being dropped by American B-52s and F-15s, the thunderclap of the explosions reaching them long after they saw the flares.

The next day the Canadians continued climbing ridgeline to ridgeline, finding unexploded mortars, rifles, ammunition, the remnants of mortar placements and firing positions. On this day they found two bodies as well, in front of a cave, already starting to decompose, maggots feeding on the heads, birds pecking away and stubbornly refusing to be scared off. The bodies were so badly decomposed it was uncertain what had actually killed them, or how long they had been there.

Inside the caves, along the ridgelines, the engineers found the detritus of military life: glossy magazines, MRE canisters (American MREs, surprisingly, and they wondered how the rebels came to have them). There were cigarette butts, clay pipes, tattered blankets, pamphlets that had been dropped by coalition aircraft warnings of what would happen to the rebels if they continued fighting. The charred remains of the pamphlets were often found inside firepits, used as kindling.

They found Pepsi bottles as well, and more than one soldier paused when they found them, looking at the Arabic script around the familiar swirling logo. They tried to imagine how such a thing would look — an al Qaeda fighter sitting by his firepit, smoking a clay pipe and drinking a Pepsi. They marched away thinking the world moved in mysterious ways, and maybe there really was more in heaven and earth than what was known of in the latest intelligence reports.

At mid-afternoon on the second day, a recce section neared the castle-like outcrop that was the peak of the Whale. From 200 metres below the summit the recce section saw a man sitting in front of a cave.

Perhaps the pinnacle had been hard to hit, or perhaps no one could fathom why you would have a bunker so far from the valley, so they didn't even bother trying to hit it. However it came to pass, there was a man sitting at the top of the mountain and the recce section quickly took cover and radioed for infantry troops. The nearest soldiers were with the American Mountain Division and it took them two hours to arrive. When they got there a plan was devised. With the Canadians covering their flank, the American soldiers lined up to the left of the cave entrance and, upon a command from their platoon commander, fired anti-tank missiles through the cave entrance.

This was followed by a barrage of light and heavy machine-gun cover, while American soldiers moved over the rock formation, firing their guns down "spider holes," the escape routes that every rebel bunker had, and which were now made clearly visible by the smoke rising from the ground. After that fragmentation grenades were dropped down the holes.

When the assault was over, the soldiers inched carefully toward the cave. They found two bodies lying near the cave entrance, while inside they found a cache of mortar rounds, rocket-propelled grenades, small-arms munitions, food, and medical supplies, including intravenous packets suspended from the ceiling. It was one of the largest bunkers the Canadians would find on the Whale.

* * *

Marc Léger made it to the Whale. He wasn't going to miss Canada's first combat mission since the Korean War, even if he was working in the storeroom and should have been helping Wayne Green with the airlift supply line. When a soldier in A Company sprained his ankle the day before the mission, Marc volunteered to take his place. Because of his experience and size — he was a man who could make his way up and down a mountain easily enough — the offer was readily accepted.

He spent four days on the Whale, sleeping on ridgelines, eating MREs morning, noon, and night, boiling the water on a small stove he kept in his rucksack. He found caves — plenty of caves — each time wondering if an enemy combatant was inside, approaching carefully, like he had been trained. The hard tingling on his skin as he approached, the shallow breathing, it was the physical manifestation of anticipating something, of fearing and welcoming something at the same time. A march in the ranks hard-prest, and the road unknown. In those four days Marc Léger came as close to being a soldier as he would ever come.

Soldiers during Operation Harpoon struggle up the steep slopes in the mountainous region near Gardez. At a height of 9,000 feet, oxygen levels are low and troops are forced to stop and rest frequently in order to carry on the long hike to the top.

Sean Hackett would remember seeing him marching down a ridgeline, his bulky frame blocking out the soldiers coming up behind him. The commander would be surprised to see him, his stores-man, out humping with the rest of the jumpers. He asked how he came to be there and Marc told him about the soldier with the sprained ankle, then started talking about the ride on the Black Hawk, the chopper flying in just over what would have been a low treeline, if there were any trees on this mountain, the caves he had found, the mortar emplacements and fortified bunkers, blown up by engineers, so they'd never be used again.

Then he walked away, bearing an almost childish smile. Hackett remembers it well, the way you tend to when a big man is so filled with happiness it shows right on the contours of his face.

Other than the two men at the summit of the Whale, Canadian soldiers would find no other rebel fighters during Operation Harpoon. They would, however, find and clear forty-five caves, about fifteen more than what their briefings said they would find. They never had trouble reaching the caves, despite the high altitude, the steep inclines, and the forty-five kilograms worth of kit and weapons some of the soldiers carried. Their physical training — the daily PT exercises, the exercises in the mountains of southern Alberta — had worked. More than once they had come to the aid of an American soldier who had sprained an ankle, or been left exhausted along a switchback, unable to continue.

"Something big is in store for us," Stogran told the soldiers before they boarded the Black Hawks back to Bagram. "We demonstrated to the Americans that we exceed expectations and we will exceed expectation in everything we do."

Not that he was completely happy with the mission. On the second day, a platoon-section with the American Mountain Division had called in an air strike on what they thought were rebel fighters, but actually were Princess Patricia's. The strike was called off at the last possible moment and Stogran was still seething at the mistake. He complained to NDHQ about the Mountain Division, saying the American soldiers on the Whale were nothing like the Task Force Rakkasan soldiers. In poor shape and inadequately prepared for the mission, Stogran refused to be deployed with the Mountain Division again, saying he would rather return to Canada then expose his soldiers to risk of an accidental air attack.

CHAPTER FOURTEEN

Back in Canada it had been reported that Canadian soldiers had deployed on the country's first combat mission since the Korean War. For the first few days back at the Kandahar Airfield, most of the soldiers were busy trying to get phone or computer time, so they could tell their families everything was all right. They were back in camp.

After that life at the airfield settled into a steady, almost monotonous routine. The rush of arriving in Afghanistan back in February, working with the 101st Airborne, going on Operation Harpoon, all that faded during the last weeks of March, replaced with repetitive days that saw the soldiers rotate from the line to administrative and security tasks at the terminal to downtime in their tents, where they would try to escape the midday heat by sleeping, writing letters home, or catching scorpions.

Courtesy of Combat Camera

Sergeant Mark Pennie on top of his reverse osmosis water machine.

Living conditions improved during this time. Pennie's water-purification machine was up and running, so the three-litres-of-water-a-day ration was lifted. The machine stopped much of the grumbling by the Americans as well, many of whom were still upset that the Canadians had taken the place of one of their rifle companies. Pennie's machine was the only one working at the airfield. The American machines had broken down in the first two weeks.

The Canadian engineer started providing bottled water for all of Task Force Rakkasan, while at the same time examining the ancient plumbing in the terminal, wondering if there was a way of repairing it, perhaps getting some toilets and showers working. The shitcans were probably the biggest complaint in both the American and Canadian camps, more loathed than even the MREs.

Wayne Green started putting a decent regimental storeroom together, with everything under tarps or some sort of jerry-rigged walls and ceiling. His desk had been right out in the open for the first few weeks, the regimental quartermaster was too busy to do anything about it, or care much, even when the American troops had started laughing at him — the little orphaned quartermaster.

Alex Watson and the engineers were making progress with their schools, several were up and running by mid-April. The battalion distributed school supplies when they arrived and Stogran or Borland would often visit a village when a school officially opened, to meet the elders, asking what else needed to be done and if any Taliban fighters were in the area, which would make it difficult for the Canadians to continue helping the village.

By April, Stogran had also made arrangements for four-day R&R trips to Dubai to begin. In a lot of little ways, life was getting easier in Afghanistan.

Training exercises were a constant. Not only were they a way to keep the soldiers' skills from atrophying, it helped break up the boredom of what was becoming a steady three-part duty rotation — from the line to the terminal to your tent.

There were drills mimicking a mortar attack on the line. Or a platoon section attack on the line. In PT, soldiers spent more time than usual grappling, going skin-to-skin with another soldier, even though there had been no reports — at least none that the 3rd Battalion knew about — of any unarmed combat between coalition forces and the Taliban.

Some of the training was done off base, at a place called Tarnak Farm. Here the soldiers could practise with their weapons. Along with the Browning 9-mm pistols and C-7 assault rifles that most soldiers carried, the battalion had brought over C-6, C-8, and C-9 machines guns, as well as heavier weapons like the 84-mm Carl Gustav recoilless rifle, some Eryx anti-armour guns, as well as the TOW, your classic bunker-buster, anti-tank missile weapon.

The Canadians had started with small training exercises at Tarnak Farm — platoon-section level, mostly small-arms fire — but had gradually started to increase the size and complexity. The range was only fourteen kilometers from the airfield, a hundred acres with lots of old tanks scattered around that could be used as targets. The place couldn't have been designed any better.

In early April the battle group started organizing a company-strength training exercise at Tarnak Farm. This would be a live-fire exercise; two exercises run at the same time, both simulating an attack on the line. A Company was going to be deployed in late April to the Khost Airfield, giving American Marines there an opportunity to leave the line and go to Dubai on their own R&R break. Khost is in Eastern Afghanistan, all of fourteen kilometres from the Pakistani border, and considered a "hot area." There were al Qaeda and Taliban fighters in the mountains surrounding the village and the airfield had recently been attacked with rocket-propelled grenades and small-arms fire. There was a good chance the Canadians would see combat in Khost.

The company's second-in-command, Captain Joe Jasper, made a request for the training range to the battle group's training officer, who presented it at the weekly Task Force Rakkasan resource meeting. Both the Canadians and Americans shared the range, and any request had to make its way up the American command chain.

Jasper's request outlined the training exercise the company wanted to undertake. It would be a nighttime exercise, two run at the same time. One exercise would simulate a small-arms firefight. The other would replicate a platoon-size ambush on Canadian infantry soldiers. The request gave the list of weapons that would be used — C-6, C-7, C-8, and C-9 machine guns, pistols, shotguns, and the Carl Gustav recoilless rifle.

The following week the Americans approved the request. A Company had Tarnak Farm booked for the night of April 17th.

PART III
Tarnak Farm

In every trade save war men of talent and vigor prosper.
In war they die.

— Cormac McCarthy, *The Crossing*

If a forest catches fire, both the dry and the wet will burn.

— Afghan Proverb

They drove along the coastline of St. Margaret's Bay, through Frenchtown, Indianhead, Seabright, making their way to Peggy's Cove, where the ashes of Private Nathan Smith had been cast to the wind.

Stogran stared at the ocean, the waves cresting and falling on the rocky shoreline, a flock of seagulls circling a small trawler rolling out on the horizon. In Afghanistan the birds tended to be carrions, crows and vultures, big black birds that dotted the sky. The Taliban used the birds to locate coalition patrols, they circled wherever there was a chance of food. The coalition — all right, the Americans — had drones that would locate enemy forces. The Taliban had the birds.

What can you say about an enemy that uses birds as a recce patrol? That's force-of-nature shit.

They reached Peggy's Cove, parked, and then climbed the steps to the lighthouse, the RSM, his wife, and the escort officer walking ahead of him. Stogran assumed Smith's ashes would have been spread from the lighthouse, from the tallest point of land, although he wasn't sure. That detail hadn't been in the briefing booklet.

When they stood at the base of the lighthouse, it looked just the way it did in postcards. Sometimes when you see something for real, after only seeing photos or what have you, you're disappointed. The photos have made it look better, or different, than what it actually is. But not the lighthouse at Peggy's Cove. It looked the way it was supposed to, a sturdy beacon turned to the Atlantic Ocean, surrounded by rock beaten flat by wind and salt and time.

He wondered for a moment if there were two places on the planet more different than the coastline of Nova Scotia and the desert of Afghanistan. They had nothing in common. No natural link. But the two places had been joined because of military treaties and politics, although that was so often the course of history Stogran could not muster the effort to act surprised.

He took one last look around and then trudged down the path to the parking lot. So both Smith and Green had been Nova Scotia boys. They must have hated Kandahar.

* * *

Nathan's dad was a captain on a fuel boat in the Halifax Harbour, a sea captain just like Nathan's grandfather had been. His grandfather had piloted a bum boat around the Halifax Harbour for fifty years, supplying dry goods to boats that had sailed into port, never got captain's papers, but when he went to sea back in the thirties no one asked a bum-boat captain if they had papers.

Lloyd Smith worked the same ships, only he gave them fuel instead of provisions. He spent a lot of years with Imperial Oil, then Algoma Tankers when Imperial sold the business. With a background like that, Smith still wondered why his son didn't become a sailor when he enlisted. But Nathan had asked to be infantry, and as soon as he became infantry he wanted to become a jumper. It still made no sense to his father.

"He loved jumping out of planes," Smith said as they sat in the living room of his farmhouse in Tatamagouche. "I could never figure that out, because Nathan was scared of heights. He hated climbing up a ladder."

No figuring some things, Smith supposed. Why would a boy who had saltwater almost running through his veins, who went to school to

Courtesy of Department of National Defence

Private Nathan Smith.

become a commercial diver — finishing top of his class at Seneca College — why a boy like that would end up a soldier? Well, it's true what they say about life being a mystery. Go mad trying to keep track of all the crazy things zipping by you most days.

Smith had booked off work when he had been contacted and asked if he would mind if a party from the Edmonton Garrison came to visit him; Nathan's commander wanted to meet him. He sat on the couch in his living room with his wife, Charlotte, the couple leaning forward slightly, expectant looks on their faces. It was obviously Stogran's lead.

"I wanted to come and meet you, tell you how sorry I am about what happened to Nathan," he said, putting down his teacup. "He should have come home. It was my job to bring him home."

"I don't see what you could have done different, from what I've read in the papers," said Smith.

"It's a commander's job to bring everyone home, Mr. Smith. It's the most important part of the job. The reasons why you fail, they don't matter all that much."

"Well, I appreciate you coming out to see us," his wife said. "Will you be visiting all the families?"

"Yes, ma'am."

"That's going to be hard on you."

Did she just say that? Hard on him? Stogran would be home in two days with his wife and two children, putting Afghanistan behind him. What he was doing right now, it was simply his duty. Hard had nothing to do with it. They drank their tea and then Lloyd Smith said, "I have something I want to show you. Come, follow me."

The air outside smelled of salt and fish, the Northumberland Strait not that far away, the French and Waugh rivers even closer. The men from the Edmonton Garrison stood with the Smiths, looking at three flagpoles that had been erected next to the century-old farmhouse. At the top of one mast was the Canadian flag. On the second were the regimental colours of the Princess Patricia's. On the last, the insignia for Alpha Company.

"Where did you get the flags?" asked Stogran.

"They came back with Nathan," said Smith.

Charlotte Smith spoke then, saying she wasn't sure at first whether it was a good idea, raising the three flags next to their home, wondered if it would be a daily reminder of losing Nathan when there were already enough reminders of that. Why add one more? But once he had been given the flags her husband was determined. Everyone, she supposed, grieved in different ways.

It kept him busy: digging the holes, pouring the cement, getting the poles just right. He had not stopped there. Was building a picket fence, it was already half complete, and there would be flowers in beds, and more in boxes around the poles. A lot of work, and maybe that was a good thing. When her husband came back from sea, it gave him something to do.

She talked as though nervous, as though explaining something she feared might seem an obsession. When she finished her husband turned to Stogran and said simply, "So what actually happened that day?"

CHAPTER FIFTEEN

Al Jaber Air Base, Kuwait

Major Harry Schmidt arrived in Kuwait on March 16, 2002, with the second wave of the U.S. 170 Expeditionary Fighter Squadron. The fighter pilot came with the 183 Fighter Wing of the Illinois Air National Guard, based in Springfield, Illinois.

Schmidt would be one more pilot in the complicated military mix that was Operation Enduring Freedom. The air component of the war against terror had fighter jets, transport planes, attack choppers, air-surveillance planes, tanker planes, all under control of Coalition Air Operations Centre (CAOC), based at Prince Sultan Air Base in Al Kharj, Saudi Arabia. COAC monitored, controlled, and gave out the tasking orders for every coalition air unit in the region, including the 332nd Air Expeditionary Group, based in Al Jaber.

The 183rd Fighter Wing, while not a full-time military unit, was going to be in Al Jaber for ninety days. It was the first time since the Gulf War that an Air National Guard unit had accepted a ninety-day overseas rotation, although that was typical of the 183rd. If everyone else was going to be in for thirty, then the 183rdth would be there for sixty. If everyone else was doing sixty, then the 183th would do ninety. That was the sort of bravado that had attracted Schmidt to the fighter wing in the first place.

Born and raised in St. Louis, Missouri, Schmidt had been a star high school athlete; a tall, brawny kid who was good enough to get an athletic scholarship to the United States Naval Academy, where he was goalie for the Midshipmen's soccer team. Although he had been an average student, he went on to excel at the flight school in Pensacola, Florida, after graduating from the Naval Academy. It turned out the skills needed by an NCAA Division One soccer keeper — fast reflexes, good hand-eye coordination, an almost enraptured awareness of the playing field — were the same skills needed by a top-flight fighter pilot.

He quickly became known for his bravado and an unshakeable confidence in his own skills. One day in Pensacola, when an instructor told him to merge beside his wing, Schmidt made the manoeuvre at a high rate of speed, stopping right to the left of the instructor as easily as if he had just done a parallel park. In class the next day the instructor — in good humour, with obvious respect — called him a psycho. Soon that's what his classmates were calling him as well, "Psycho Schmidt," an alliterative nickname he would carry with him for the rest of his military career.

Once he left Pensacola, Schmidt rose quickly through the ranks. He was assigned to the USS *Kennedy*, where he flew F-18 Hornets. His first combat mission was in 1993, when he was part of Operation Deny Flight over Bosnia and Herzegovina. That same year he was assigned to the Navy's Fighter-Weapon School in San Diego — the Top Gun school made famous by Tom Cruise in the movie of the same name. Only the best of the navy's pilots were invited to the school. Schmidt was so good he was invited back two years later to be an instructor.

After his stint as a Top Gun instructor he flew combat missions in Kosovo. Then he became the navy's first exchange-instructor with the United States Air Force, getting assigned to the air force's weapons school at the Nellis Air Force Base in Nevada.

While his military career was progressing better than anyone at Annapolis might have guessed, his personal live was not so ascending. He divorced his first wife — they met while both were attending the Naval Academy — after only seven years. He met his second wife, Lisa, a navy nurse, while working out in a gym in San Diego. They quickly had two children, both boys, and Schmidt grew tired of the near-constant overseas deployments and reassignments. He began looking for a position with an Air National Guard unit, so he could spend more time with his family. It didn't take him long. The 183rd Fighter Wing in Springfield, Illinois, offered him a job in the spring of 2000, even though it would have to wait nearly eighteen months before he could report for duty. Still, the 183rd didn't mind waiting for a pilot with Schmidt's credentials. The squadron made him their full-time weapons instructor.

Schmidt moved to Illinois in December 2001 with his wife and two young sons. He built himself an opulent home on the edge of the Rail Golf Course in suburban Springfield and settled in for the good, middle years of a man's life.

Kandahar Airfield

Most of A Company spent the morning of April 17, 2002, practising a drill. There was always some sort of drill, some sort of training exercise, going on at the Canadian base. This one had the company learning how to load wounded soldiers onto American Black Hawk helicopters — in what order the wounded soldiers should be loaded and how to secure the stretchers once they were on the chopper.

The week before, part of the company had been on four days R&R in Dubai, and they were still getting re-acclimatized to Kandahar, with its scorching midday temperatures and freezing nights, its constant dust and arid landscape. In Dubai the third platoon had stayed in a four-star resort with a swim-up bar and discotheque, right on the beach, just a few blocks from some of the best shops and restaurants in the Arabian Peninsula. Some of the soldiers never left the resort — never left the pool — but others took advantage of the shops. They bought school supplies for Alex Watson, presents for family back in Edmonton.

Ricky Green, a young private in the platoon's 3rd section, spent most of his time looking for an engagement ring for his girlfriend. He went from shop to shop until he found one he liked. After that he showed it to some of the soldiers in his section, the soldiers saying he had done well, she'll love it Ricky. He told his friends he was going to propose as soon as he got home — probably the first night. Didn't think he could wait. He asked some of the other soldiers, the ones in his section who were already engaged, how they had done it. What's the best way to propose? As though doing it once made you an expert. Green was only twenty-one, one of the youngest soldiers in the platoon, and his last name was unfortunate, although many of the guys in the platoon thought they would have nick-named him "Greener" no matter what he'd been christened.

They gave him advice as best they could. Ainsworth Dyer, a giant of a man from the tough Regent Park neighbourhood of Toronto, told him how he had proposed to his fiancée on a bridge in Edmonton, after a romantic dinner. Dyer said bridges were good for proposals. If his girlfriend had said no, he would have thrown her over. At least, that's what he told her later.

Nathan Smith, another engaged soldier, said he should do it the old-fashioned way, dropping to one knee and offering her the ring. Smith was the same rank as Green but five years older. He'd knocked around some before joining the army, been to community college, used to play in a rock band. All the other privates in the platoon looked up to him.

Maybe Smith was right, thought Green. Dropping to one knee seemed a better option than going to a bridge with a backup plan.

Marc Léger spent the morning in the A Company storeroom, then began his lunch run to the line. It was part of his daily routine, driving a truck to the observations posts, bringing out the MREs. He didn't much like being in the storeroom, hoped it wouldn't become a long-term posting, although he enjoyed driving around, talking to the rest of the battalion. With most jobs you only had contact with your platoon, sometimes just your section.

After the lunch run he made his way to the terminal, where he was to meet an American quartermaster to do a bit of bartering. Although he didn't like being in stores, Léger was showing an aptitude for it. He was a skilled negotiator. A world-class scavenger. It was the skill-set of a good quartermaster and Léger was starting to worry slightly, wondering if he were too good would he ever get out of the storeroom? Still, if there was a job to do you might as well do it.

He traded the quartermaster some boxes of MREs for some plywood. The Yanks loved the Canadian MREs, which showed you how bad they had it. He'd use the plywood to make a floor in the storeroom to get everything off the pallets. Before leaving the American base he also took a look at a badly damaged Soviet Jeep, to see if there was anything he could salvage. He had been building a weight room for the company, a *Pee-wee Herman's Playhouse* sort of affair, with tire rims for the weights, drive-shafts for the bars. If he had enough plywood he'd put down a floor there as well. He was also thinking of building some more tables for the television tent. The first round of the NHL playoffs had begun, and the tent was getting crowded some nights.

Sadly, he found the Jeep had already been stripped, as had a couple of trucks nearby that he thought could be scavenged. He headed back to the Canadian base with just the lumber to show for his efforts. Still, it had been a good foraging trip. Lumber was at a premium on the airfield.

When he got back to the Canadian base he used the storeroom computer to send a quick email to his wife.

> I just received your email … boy, do I ever miss you. I wish I could spend more time writing you. Everyone is sharing the one computer, except all the officers, they have their own.
>
> I love you very much, and now that I have your [email] address I will write as much as possible.

> Love Marc

Al Jaber Air Base

Schmidt awoke at 10:30 a.m. that morning and looked out on another bright, hot day. In seven hours he would be flying a night mission over Afghanistan, and although he had hoped to sleep in longer, the heat and the sun made it impossible.

He would be the wingman for the flight that night, not the lead, and when he saw the posting the night before he had been surprised. The lead would be William Umbach, whose full-time job was flying jumbo jets for American Airlines. Schmidt had no complaints about Umbach. He was a former Air Force pilot who had more than 1,500 hours in the cockpit of an F-16, more than 3,000 cockpit hours in total, so the man was more than qualified. He was an instructor pilot, just like Schmidt.

Still, Umbach's combat experience had been limited. He certainly didn't have the experience of Schmidt. He had been a reservist for more than a decade, becoming the squadron commander in 1998 — which made sense, the man was known for his organizational skills, was well-liked by everyone in the squadron — but flying lead, with a Top Gun pilot as his wingman? Schmidt thought the posting was strange enough to ask whether there had been a mistake.

No mistake. He would be the wingman.

After getting out of bed, Schmidt took some clothes to the laundry, then walked to the mess for lunch. He had been in Kuwait for a month, had flown seven missions but seen no action. Nor had any pilot with the 183rd. Two days earlier a squadron pilot had released a bomb, but it had missed the target. Other than that, their missions had been defensive counter-air and interdiction missions over Iraq, or on-call close air support and on-call interdiction missions over Afghanistan. Which meant you went up and waited for something to happen.

They had missed Operation Anaconda by days. That would have been real action, a full-bore air assault on the Shah-i-Kot Valley. Coalition forces had been surprised by the number of Taliban and al Qaeda fighters in the area, so the air campaign had gone on for days. Taliban commander Maulvi Saif-ur Mansur had even been reported in the area, the dictionary definition of a high-value target. Anaconda had been the first large-scale battle in Afghanistan since Toro Bora back the previous December. Now Operation Enduring Freedom seemed to be at a standstill.

In the mess hall some pilots were still talking about the failed bombing mission two days before. It had been against a mobile artillery target in northern Iraq, a target that had moved before the pilots arrived, but they didn't realize that and had released the bomb. After lunch Schmidt stopped at the medical clinic and asked the pharmacist for some go and no-go pills.

The no-go pills were sleeping tablets, the go pills were Dexedrine, issued regularly to air force pilots. The navy had never used them and even the air force had banned them after the Gulf War, but then they'd started up again when they went into the Balkans. Air force fighter pilots had to fly up to twelve hours in the cramped cockpits of the F-16s, and fatigue had killed a lot of good pilots. The go pills seemed a safer alternative, even though they were classified as a Schedule II narcotic by the U.S. Food and Drug Administration. Schmidt took the plastic baggie of pills and went to his quarters. There wouldn't be enough time for an afternoon nap.

Kandahar Airfield

While Léger was on the computer, Sergeant Craig Reid and Major Sean Hackett came into the storeroom. There were always soldiers in the storeroom, it was where the computers were, where you came when you needed something, where card games were played late at night. While

Léger finished his email to Marley he heard the two men talking about a problem with a training exercise that night.

The next week, A Company was going to be deployed to the Khost Airfield to man the line there. Hackett had been told his troops could expect combat while in Khost. It was a "hot area." The line at Kandahar was also seeing some action those days. Just the week before there had been an exchange of small-arms fire on the northeast edge of the line, the first since several such incidents back in February and early March. The attacks were always at night, so A Company was going on a live-ammo training exercise that night. The problem? Reid was supposed to be one of the safety officers for the training exercise, but he had paperwork he needed to finish for Hackett.

Léger listened to the debate — what's more important, the paperwork or Reid going on the training exercise? There are only so many soldiers trained to be safety officers, so Reid wanted to blow off the paperwork, but the company commander wasn't happy it was boiling down to a one-or-the-other solution.

"Hey, Craig," said Léger, after hitting the send button, "I can take your place on the range tonight."

"Are you sure?" asked Reid.

"Sure. It will get me out of the storeroom."

Al Jaber Air Base

Schmidt and Umbach attended a pilots' meeting and listened to a rehash of the failed bombing mission two days ago. It had been the first time the 170th squadron had pushed the "pickle button" — the button that released a bomb — and the lead pilot on the flight described what happened, how his wingman had spotted what he thought was the mobile target, then released a bomb that missed by 150 feet. Turned out he wasn't even looking at the right target. To make the flight a complete disaster — and it was already pretty close — Major-General Walter Buchanan, commander of Joint Task Force Southwest Asia, had been at Al Jaber the day it happened.

After the pilots' meeting, Schmidt and Umbach headed directly to their mission briefing. They watched briefing slides on what they could expect on the mission and what they should be aware of. As part of the presentation there were maps of Afghanistan showing the Kandahar Airfield as a "friendly airfield," a place that coalition pilots could use in case they needed to make an emergency landing.

There were other slides showing that Taliban forces south of Kandahar might be in possession of surface-to-air missiles smuggled in from Iran. The missiles were called "ringbacks," 122-mm multiple-rocket launchers modified for use as surface-to-air missiles, with a maximum altitude of 56,000 feet. (In a briefing the previous week, one of the slides contained information on a Navy Seal who had been caught, tortured, and shot by suspected al Qaeda fighters, near Kandahar.)

The briefing did not contain information on a training exercise at Tarnak Farm that night, even though the information had been passed along to Coalition Air Operations Centre. The omission was not surprising. The previous month, coalition pilots had complained about too much information being given to them during mission briefings. The Airspace Control Order (ACO) was starting to run to fifty pages or more. The in-flight computer maps were getting so confusing — with all the information that had to be inputted from the ACOs — they were practically unreadable. The ACO had been severely truncated since then, the maps simplified.

As the briefing ended, that night's flight was given a code name. It would be called "Coffee Flight." Umbach would be "Coffee 51," Schmidt would be "Coffee 52."

The pilots were driven to their planes, F-16s built by Lockheed Martin, the fastest jets at the Al Jaber Air Base. Each was equipped with four 500-pound GBUs (guided bomb units), two under each wing. Both pilots climbed into the cockpits of the F-16s and started final checks. After twenty minutes, Umbach took off down the runway, followed less than a minute later by Schmidt.

To avoid Iranian airspace the pilots took nearly four hours to reach their on-call station area, a map grid in the northeastern corner of Afghanistan. The sky was clear, with scattered clouds at 8,000 feet and 20,000 feet, and upper level winds from the west at between twenty and forty knots. A perfect night for flying.

Afghanistan Airspace

Five hours before Coffee Flight reached its patrol area in Afghanistan, a twenty-one-man American Airborne Warning and Control Systems (AWACS) flight also took off. Working out of a converted Boeing 707 rigged up with state-of-the-art radar and communications systems, the AWACS monitored air traffic over Afghanistan, coordinated mid-air refuelling for the fighters, and acted as a liaison between pilots and the Coalition Air Operations Center. After reaching its cruising altitude, the AWACS crew, on its tenth mission in Afghanistan, began systems checks. The plane was on station, all systems checked and verified, by 5:30 p.m., about fifteen minutes ahead of schedule.

The air force officer who would be talking to COFFEE FLIGHT that night was Tech-Sergeant Michael Carroll. He also had been given a call signal — BOSSMAN.

CHAPTER SIXTEEN

Tarnak Farm

If it were possible, it seemed hotter than it had been at noon. The soldiers from A Company sat in the shade of the trucks, wiping sweat from their faces, complaining about having to go on their second exercise of the day. Shortly after 3:00 p.m. the convoy — five American medium-logistics trucks, an ambulance, some Iltis Jeeps, two Coyotes as escort — set out for the fourteen-kilometre drive to the range.

Like most things in Afghanistan, Tarnak Farm had a former life. It had once been a fruit orchard and there were many dried-up streams and irrigation ditches — called wadis — crisscrossing the hundred-acre property. The soldiers had been to the training range many times since arriving in Afghanistan, but could still not imagine a time when this was anything but arid desert.

Tarnak Farm had also been one of the largest al Qaeda training facilities in Afghanistan before Operation Enduring Freedom began — the place where Osama bin Laden trained hundreds of Jihadists. Tarnak Farm is where bin Laden recorded a video message after the September 11 attacks, threatening retribution against the United States and its allies if Afghanistan were invaded. It is the place where American intelligence reports had placed the terrorist leader many times. More than once the United States military had considered an attack on the former fruit orchard, always deciding against it for fear of civilian deaths.

Coalition bombing had reduced most of the buildings at Tarnak Farm to rubble, but the walls of the former stables where bin Laden had kept his horses, and the nearly eighty houses where his followers once lived, were still standing. The convoy parked beside what was left of the corral, to keep the vehicles in the shade. An administration area was set up, as was an area where the ammunition would be dispensed to soldiers as they headed out to the range. Léger's boss, Warrant-Officer Billy Bolen, would be in charge of the ammunition area.

There would be two training exercises running at the same time that night, both using wadis that intersected to form a near-perfect *L*, one dried-up stream bed running east to west, the other north to south. The north-south wadi would be a close-quarter range, under the supervision of Captain Joe Jasper. The other would be a tank-stalk range, under supervision of Marc Léger.

The close-quarter range would have small groups of soldiers, two to five at a time, making their way down the wadi using small arms — pistols and shotguns — to fire at pop-up targets as they appeared above them. The exercise would end when they reached the end of the wadi.

Soldiers on the tank-stalk range would be doing a larger, more complicated drill. Here, a platoon section, seven soldiers bolstered by a two-man C-6 machine-gun unit, would march down the wadi until they encountered a pop-up target on its left ridge. After the lead soldier had taken down the target, the rest of the section would charge up the wadi, assume firing positions along the top, and begin an attack on several old Soviet tanks a few hundred yards away. The attack would be aided by the C-6 machine gun and am 84-mm Carl Gustav recoilless rifle, which would be firing rounds toward the tanks.

When the Canadians arrived, U.S. Army Rangers were on the range, and it took half an hour for them to complete their exercise and pack up. After that, Canadian pioneers went to work getting the pop-up targets into position. When the pioneers gave the all-clear, Léger and Jasper inspected the ranges, telling Hackett shortly after 4:00 p.m. that everything was ready and the exercise could begin. Because all the soldiers had their watches set to Zulu Time, which is four-and-a-half hours ahead of local time in Afghanistan, it was already getting dark when the exercises began. Before long the only light in the sky was the tracer rounds coming from the tank-stalk range.

Coffee Flight

Schmidt and Umbach flew over northeastern Afghanistan, cruising at an altitude of 22,000 feet. Except for the stars, there were few lights either around or below them as they patrolled one of the most desolate stretches of Afghanistan airspace. The next day's report would say what it always did: "No significant events occurred during the scheduled period of flight; the flight was not tasked to deploy any weapons; the flight returned to base on schedule."

Shortly after takeoff, Schmidt had taken two of his go pills. Umbach had taken one. The mission was scheduled to last for ten hours and it was difficult to stay alert sometimes, especially given the repetitive nature of the work. Check on-board computers. Check on-board maps. Stare at a black sky. Repeat. Since the Vietnam War, fatigue had killed more fighter pilots than enemy fire.

Near the end of their patrol, Umbach radioed the AWACS and spoke with BOSSMAN to arrange an in-air refuelling. The AWACS controller gave the lead pilot the coordinates for the tanker, telling the pilots to depart southwest on a compass heading of 230 degrees. It was a flight path that would take them directly over the Tarnak Farm.

The 3rd section of the 3rd platoon gathered in the administration area, waiting for its turn to go out on the tank-stalk range. The section was under the command of Sergeant Lorne Ford, a former member of the disbanded Airborne Regiment. Ford is a tough, no-nonsense soldier who has a reputation for leading his section no matter the drill or the mission, although that night he had given command to his second-in-command so he could observe and see how his unit performed. Master-Corporal Stanley Clark, a thirty-five-year-old Vancouver native, was second-in-command.

A platoon section doesn't have commissioned officers. It is normally in command of a sergeant, with master-corporals, corporals, and privates taking orders. These are your enlisted soldiers, the men and women who never went to Royal Roads or Royal Military College, who didn't join the army to get a university degree or work their way up the command chain at National Defence Headquarters. The soldiers in the 3rd section are typical of most infantry sections.

The corporals were Brett Perry and Brian Decaire, two PT junkies who often worked in extra exercise in Kandahar by running up and down the airfield runway. The section had two other corporals, René Paquette, who came over from the 2nd Battalion, based in Winnipeg, when a call for volunteers went out after the battle group came up a couple dozen soldiers short. Paquette's wife had given birth to a baby girl two weeks earlier. The other corporal was Chris Oliver, who would not be on the range that night as his weapon, an M-230 grenade launcher, was not part of the exercise. The private in the section, and also the youngest member, was Ricky Green.

Joining the section on the training range was a two-man C-6 machine-gun unit. Corporal Ainsworth Dyer was firing the gun. He had enlisted when he was seventeen, stood a head taller than just about everyone else in Alpha Company, and competed regularly in the garrison's annual Mountain Man competition, a fifty-kilometre hike and canoe trek where participants carry a fifteen-kilogram rucksack as they run and paddle. One year he competed with two stress fractures in his left leg. Because of his size and stamina, Dyer was a natural choice to operate the C-6 machine gun, a weapon three feet long and weighing close to twenty pounds. The weapon is so big it takes two soldiers to operate, one firing, one feeding a linked belt of ammunition into the gun. The soldier loading the gun that night was Private Nathan Smith.

The soldiers, along with Master-Corporal Curtis Hollister, commander of the weapons detachment, waited for the signal to go out on the tank-stalk range and begin the exercise. Some of them had tried to get some sleep earlier, but it had been a failed exercise. It was difficult to run drills like this back in Canada — there were so many rules and regulations governing live fire — so it was exciting, getting out on a range and simulating a real combat mission. It was noisy as hell too, what with the machine guns and the Gustav. The soldiers had resigned themselves to just a few hours of sleep when they got back to base. Hopefully they could get caught back up the next night.

Finally, shortly after 9:00 p.m., the section was called out to the tank-stalk range, where Léger was waiting to brief them. He quickly outlined the drill: A force of about fifty al Qaeda fighters were planning an attack on the Kandahar Airfield. They were armed and highly motivated, and would fight to the death. The pop-up target — when the section saw it — would be the first sighting of the rebel force. They were to take out the target, then rush to the top of the wadi to engage the rest of the combatants, who would be — here Léger pointed to the rusted-out hull of a Russian T-55 — right over there. The C-6 machine gun and the Gustav were to be used on the tank, as well as the smaller machine guns, the C-9s.

Léger asked if there any questions, but there were none. The soldiers climbed into the wadi and assumed their positions. At 9:17 Léger gave the all-clear-sign and Clark signalled for the exercise to begin.

CHAPTER SEVENTEEN

Coffee Flight

Schmidt and Umbach flew over Tarnak Farm and saw the gunfire below. Perhaps the briefing slides back at Al Jaber — the ones talking about rattlebacks — came to the pilots' minds, or perhaps after a month of monotonous, near-uniform missions, the fire below was so out of place, so extraordinary, they gave it an import it did not deserve. Perhaps, as Schmidt would claim months later, the go pills had simply impaired his judgment. Whatever the reason, upon seeing the live-fire exercise at Tarnak Farm, both pilots thought they were seeing surface-to-air fire (SAFIRE).

They radioed the AWACS to report what they were seeing, then started getting a map coordinate on where the fire was originating. At 9:22.38 p.m. both pilots activated their in-flight voice recorders, which had been turned off for the flight back to Al Jaber.

The first recorded message came from Umbach, who said to Schmidt: "Do you have good co-ordinate for a mark or ya need me to roll in?"

Schmidt replied: "Uhh, standby, I'll mark it right now."

Less than a minute later, Schmidt radioed the AWACS controller to say: "I've got a tally on the vicinity. I, ah, request permission to lay down some, uh, twenty mike mike."

Schmidt had just asked permission to fire his 20-mm guns. He was still not sure what he was looking at, and Umbach replied with the only caution the lead pilot would issue that night: "Let's just make sure that it's, uh, that it's not friendlies is all."

BOSSMAN quickly turned down the request to open fire, telling Schmidt to "standby." The controller found the request unusual. Schmidt would have to descend well below safe altitude to fire the guns — the last thing he should do if he believed he was under fire. As well, it would be a serious breach of standing orders for any coalition jet fighter. If under attack, they are supposed to leave the area and wait for orders from Coalition Air Operations Center.

After telling Schmidt to standby, BOSSMAN radioed Coalition Air Control Centre to speak to the commanding officer on duty, telling him: "Coffee 51 flight has experienced SA fire near the city of Kandahar, requesting permission to open up with 20 mm. I'll try to get you a little more information, we told them to hold fire."

CAOC requested more information on what the pilots believe to be surface-to-air fire, and confirmed that BOSSMAN should tell them to hold fire. While this was happening, Schmidt was getting impatient. Although only seventy-nine seconds had passed since he asked permission to fire his 20-mm guns, he asked the AWACS controller if he should change his radio frequency, believing the delay in granting permission might be because of communications problems.

BOSSMAN didn't bother responding. Instead, at 9:25 he radioed Schmidt to say: "Hold fire, need details on SAFIRE for (coalition air operations control)."

Schmidt responded by saying: "Okay, I've got, uh, I've got some men on a road and it looks like a piece of artillery firing at us" — and then, so quickly the radio transcript records it as a single utterance — "I am rolling in in self-defence."

Tarnak Farm

The soldiers on the tank-stalk range were nearing the completion of the drill. They had taken out the pop-up target and were lying along the lip of the wadi, firing machine guns. Dyer and Green were roughly half-way in the line of soldiers, with Léger behind them and Hollister beside Léger. Green and Ford were to the south of the C-6 machine gun. To the north was Clark, and Decaire and Perry were at the far end of the line with the Gustav.

Léger was standing so he could get a look at the complete range. It was a moonless night, and because of the darkness the tracers — phosphorescent bullets that fire every fifth round — were brighter than normal. Léger looked up and down the line at the soldiers illuminated by the gunfire, and waited for Clark to signal the end of the exercise.

Coffee Flight

Now that Schmidt had declared self-defence, he no longer needed permission from BOSSMAN or Coalition Air Operations Command to fire his weapons. He and Umbach started targeting the soldiers on the training range, preparing to drop one of the GBUs. His request to open fire with the 20-mm guns seemed to have been forgotten.

"Check master arm," said Umbach, referring to one of the computer checks Schmidt needed to complete before releasing the bomb. "Check laser arm and check you are not in mark."

Schmidt: "I'm in from the southwest."

Umbach: "Do you show him on a bridge?"

Schmidt: "Bomb's away, cranking left."

Eight seconds after this transmission, COAC radioed the AWACS to say: "BOSSMAN, be advised that Kandahar has friendlies, you are to get COFFEE 51 out of there as soon as possible."

BOSSMAN replied: "Roger, we'll get him out of there right now."

At that precise second Schmidt sent a one-word transmission to the AWACS, a transmission so short it was missed by BOSSMAN and everyone else on the plane.

"Shack," he said, giving the signal for a direct hit on a target.

The GBU-12 Pathway is a laser-guided munitions weighing 500 pounds with a 192-pound warhead of Tritonal (80 percent TNT and 20 percent aluminum powder). The aluminum powder is used because it increases the total heat output of the TNT — sort of like souping up your car with nitrogen. The bomb has a range of eight nautical miles and a circular error probable (CEP) of 3.6 feet.

It took twenty-one seconds for the bomb to land and detonate. It was enough time for Lorne Ford to hear a whistling sound approaching him, what he would later describe as "something right out of a movie." Not everyone heard it. Just as not everyone heard the two F-16s passing overhead, although some would say later that they heard something high above them, the sky just too dark to let them know what it was.

Twenty-one seconds is not a lot of time, although it was just enough for Ford to realize his section was about to be hit with incoming fire. If anyone else understood, it was likely Léger.

As the safety officer, Léger was watching everything on the range. He was standing, looking around, not lying on the ground with all his attention focused on the hull of an old Russian tank, like the other soldiers.

If he heard the whistling he would have looked to the sky, and perhaps had one brief second of understanding.

PART IV
Soldiers Down

Many observers have called "friendly fire" a military fact of life — some argue that it is inevitable, especially in the evolving "network centric" style of modern Western warfare. These opinions aside, the Board strongly recommends that Canada must continue to actively engage her allies in a concerted effort to understand why and how fratricide incidents occur, with the aim of prevention and with the ultimate goal of preserving our scarce and increasingly valuable operational resources.

— Tarnak Farm Board of Inquiry, *Final Report*

Looking back, the thing that still amazes me is just how incredibly stupid it all was.

— Major Glen Zilkalns

The drive from Cornwall to Lancaster is short, and as they would be spending the afternoon on the 401, making their way to Toronto, Stogran had asked the escort officer to take the longer route, down County Road 2 and the north shore of the St. Lawrence River, so they could see something of the country. They drove through Glen Walter and Summerstown; the river refracting the early morning light and obscuring the boats so that only the top masts of the bigger sailing ships could be seen, looking from the highway like low-flying clouds.

This was the start of Upper Canada, right along this stretch of river, the place where the first United Empire Loyalists came after fleeing the rebellion in the United States. Lancaster was one of the original eight "Royal Townships." Stogran had read in the hotel room that the oldest log cabin in Ontario was nearby, in Williamstown, built in 1784. He tried to imagine a log cabin more than two hundred years old, whether it was simply good fortune that made it survive, or whether there was indeed something special about the workmanship, some attention to detail that long-ago refugee had brought to his new country. If they had more time, he would have liked to have seen it.

Alice Léger in her blue Legionnaire's jacket, standing in the doorway of the Lancaster Legion.

They had the address for Léger's grandmother and had no trouble finding the house when they reached Lancaster. The street is right in the heart of the village, which is not large. When RSM Comeau knocked on the door an elderly woman in a blue legionnaire's blazer answered. Stogran thought at first she had put the jacket on for them, but was told later she wore the jacket often. She was a volunteer, helped in the kitchen, started going to the Lancaster Legion when her grandson joined the cadets.

"Colonel Stogran," said Alice Léger, when they were seated around the small kitchen table, "can I get you something to drink?"

"That would be nice."

"Would you like a beer?"

Stogran laughed. It was not yet noon.

They had a lunch of cold-cut sandwiches, the RSM talking to the Légers about their son, a soldier he knew well. They had grappled often, both men interested in martial arts, taking their PT seriously. Stogran had had a few bouts with Léger himself, the sergeant big and quick on his feet, a tough opponent. Léger had beaten him once by grabbing his wrists and twisting them back, a move that was borderline cheating but Stogran had been impressed all the same. It had won Léger the match.

There were pictures of the sergeant in this small house: Léger with his brother and sister; in front of a Christmas tree dressed in young boys' pajamas. It occurred to Stogran that there were parts of a soldier's life you were never privy too, even if you shared a tent with them for six months. Even though he had been invited into the house, welcomed as a guest, Stogran felt like a voyeur when he stared at the photos.

After lunch they drove to St. Joseph's Parish Cemetery, where they stood in front of Léger's grave. It was a simple tombstone, the insignia for the Princess Patricia's Canadian Light Infantry, the sergeant's full name — Marc Daniel Léger — the date April 17, 2002, beneath the name.

Stogran stood there and wanted to tell them again how bad he felt, for not bringing their son, their grandson, back home, but he had already said as much back in the small house on Queen Street so he stood silent, his head bowed, eyes closed. He could hear Claire Léger sobbing and knew, with the sort of premonition you get sometimes in life, that she would have a hard time accepting the death of her son. Might never accept it. Would always be troubled by the mission in Afghanistan, looking for some sense, some practical explanation for why the soldiers had gone, what they had accomplished, some answer — expressed as surely as a numeric equation, worked out to the final sum — for why her son had not come home to her.

Friendly fire made it worse. An extra variant of stupid futility added to the equation, but he guessed it would have been just as painful if Léger had fallen on the Whale in a firefight with al Qaeda fighters. Soldiers did the same thing, so there was no shame to it. Try to ascertain what a mission produced, like you were harvesting a farmer's field, than go crazy when nothing weighed up properly. Truth was you produced the passage of time. Like just about every other pursuit invented by man.

They drove back to Lancaster, went inside Alice Léger's house for another beer, then stood around the cars and said their goodbyes. The RSM had already phoned Paul Dyer and he would be waiting for them at a restaurant in Regent Park.

Sergeant Marc Léger.

Courtesy of Department of National Defence

As they stood there the grandmother suddenly said, "I have something for your trip," and went back inside her house. When she returned she had two plastic bags of cheese curds in her hands.

"They're frozen right now, but they should thaw by the time you get to Toronto," she said. As he accepted the gift Stogran thought to himself: that's a smart woman, a smart, practical woman, a Franco-Ontario living in one of the original Royal Townships, so she probably learned to be practical a long time ago, has the survivor's gene in her, no nonsense, stick to your knitting — reminded him of her grandson.

There is a practicality to life that is sometimes lost sight of in times of tragedy. Again, no shame to it. For a while you lose all reference points, all sense of standing on firm land, and there are reasons why the grieving describe the experience in similar ways: freefalling, a bad dream, numb. It is as though you become detached from the physical world; a sort of commune, perhaps, with the dead. Stogran suspected there were professors in universities who had studied the phenomenon and had better words than his to describe that sense of falling off the edge of the world.

Some people never came back. Stogran had seen it. Soldiers are certainly in that damaged fraternity, although there are reasons, as well, why there are expressions like "soldiering on," a sentiment so common it is a cliché. You have to be practical, even in the worst of times. In Afghanistan, after Tarnak Farm, there had still been a line to protect, two more operational deployments, three more months to spend in tents spread out next to a runway.

Alice Léger seemed to understand that. Stogran thanked her for the gift, thanked Richard and Claire Léger for taking the time to meet him. He now knew, after three days in Eastern Canada, that these visits were as much for him as they were for the families. A way to journey back to the practical world.

Alice Léger had been right, too. Stogran had the sharp tang of good St. Albert's Cheese curds in his mouth by the time they reached the Gardiner Expressway.

CHAPTER EIGHTEEN

The Pathway landed closest to Dyer, Smith, and the C-6 machine gun. They were killed instantly, as was Léger, who had been standing directly behind them. Green, on the other side of the C-6, was also killed, his body sheltering the soldier nearest to him, Lorne Ford.

Every other soldier in the section was wounded, as were Corporal Shane Brennan and Private Norman Link — who were hit with flying shrapnel. In the administration area, 500 feet away, people were knocked to the ground from the concussive blast of the bomb. The detonation was seen as far away as the Kandahar Airfield control tower.

In the first seconds after the explosion, the soldiers in the administration area thought an accident must have happened. The Gustav had misfired. Someone had triggered a landmine. Then, as the soldiers picked themselves up, a dull ringing in their ears, they realized something else must have happened, something much more dire than a landmine or a misfiring anti-tank gun.

Still, no one spoke right away. It was too much to process all at once, too inexplicable, and in that silence moans could be heard coming from the darkness of the training range, a plaintive rasping that built and crescendoed until it turned to screams.

Sean Hackett figured it out first. He grabbed the radio in the ambulance, the frequency already set to the Canadian Command Post back at the airfield, and yelled: "Zero, this is One. We've just been engaged by fast air."

High above the training range, Major Schmidt sees a cloud of smoke plume on the desert floor. As he watches the smoke grow and then dissipate his radio relays another message from the AWACS controller.

"Coffee 51," the radio says, "disengage, friendlies, Kandahar."

"Copy," Schmidt says, "uhh, disengaging south."

* * *

Canadian soldiers had never been attacked by a weapon as lethal as the Pathway-12 GBU. On the training range there was absolute chaos for the first few moments, as dust swirled and wounded soldiers stumbled around in the dark. The training exercise had been conducted without lights, no headlights on the trucks, no flashlights allowed on the range. Fearing they might be under attack, the lights remained off and the paramedics who had accompanied the soldiers to the training range started to rush into the wadi, then stopped, unable to see two feet in front of them.

The range was a scene of carnage. Years ago the Canadian army ran training drills with animal parts on the range, so the soldiers would have some idea what real combat was like. The paramedics were completely unprepared as they stumbled over body parts, bloodied helmets, flak jackets. The range stayed dark for a long time, until finally the paramedics reported that it was impossible to work so flashlights were turned on.

The flashlights cut through the still-swirling dust, making the scene even more surreal. Everything the light caught was horrible — René Paquette on the lip of the wadi, vomiting blood; Lorne Ford bleeding out; someone's torso; a severed foot. Then the light moves on, and the night turns black again. There are shouted orders and curses, screams, and the moaning of men still in shock.

Twenty-thousand feet above the soldiers, there were no screams or moans, no swirling dust or flashlights piercing the night, but the situation was just as confusing.

"Coffee 51," says the AWACs controller, "I need the coordinates when able and need to know if any rounds were fired."

"Yeah," replies Schmidt. "I had one bomb dropped in the vicinity of, uh, 31 24 north, point 78 64 43 point 522. That's an estimate. Uh, if you had our general vicinity." A few second later, while waiting for the controller to get back to him, Schmidt sends another one-word transmission to Umbach. "Wow," he says.

The controller gets back to Schmidt, asking him to repeat the east coordinate.

"Yah, I'm not sure if that's accurate," Schmidt says. "I ... I don't have an accurate coordinate right now. Do you want me to go back and get you one?"

"Negative."

"Let's go back safe," says Umbach, who then adds his own one-word transmission — "Shit."

"They were definitely shooting at you," Schmidt says.

"It sure seemed like they were tracking around and everything and, ah, trying to lead," replies the lead pilot.

"Well, we had our lights on and that wasn't helping I don't think," Schmidt replies. "I had a group of guys on a road around a gun and it did not look organized, like it would be our guys."

"It seemed like it was right on a bridge, that's kinda where I was at," says Umbach.

"Nah, not quite," says Schmidt. There is a slight pause after that and then he utters the first words of doubt he has expressed all night. They come three minutes and sixteen seconds after he dropped the bomb. "I hope that was the right thing to do," he says.

"Me too," says Umbach.

Pat Stogran had gone to bed early that night, a troubled night's sleep, his tent next to the command post, hearing voices — "What are you guys using down there?" ... "Engaged by fast air" ... "Zero, do you copy?" ... "What the fuck?" — distant, questioning voices and white-noise static, none of it making any sense.

Then he was awoken by Regimental Sergeant Al Commeau, screaming at him: "Colonel, are you hearing this? We've got soldiers down." Stogran's eyes snapped open. He could clearly hear the radio in the command post, and as he swung his legs off the cot he thought to himself: "My God, that was no dream."

When he reached the command post the truck was already crowded. He heard Joe Jasper giving the command post an update on what has happened on the training range.

"We have one priority one," said Jasper, giving the medical code for a gravely injured soldier, "two priority twos, one priority three, and two priority four."

There is silence in the truck. Priority four is the lowest medical priority used by the Canadian army, but that's not a good thing. Priority four means a soldier doesn't require medical attention. They're dead.

"Get him to repeat that," yelled Stogran.

"Zero to one. Two priority four? Is that correct?"

"Two KIA (killed in action)," answered Jasper. "That is correct, zero."

Out on the range no one was sure how many soldiers have died. It was bedlam. Lorne Ford was bleeding badly. Six field dressings had been applied to his left leg, but still blood was pumping out, turning the sand around him to mud. Finally a medic applied a tourniquet. When the soldiers saw that they winced and turned away — a tourniquet is a bad sign, the futile gesture a medic makes when they are stuck having to do something, no matter how long-shot useless the situation is. Tourniquets mean a soldier is dying or about to lose a limb.

Ford was conscious during this, and says later he just kept telling himself, "Keep breathing. As long as you keep breathing, you're alive."

Corporal Paquette was also gravely wounded, covered in blood, although the medics couldn't find any shrapnel wounds when they cut off his tunic. They realized he'd been vomiting blood and worried that something bad had happened inside his body. He was having trouble breathing so they hooked him up to an oxygen tank. Hollister bore the brunt of the concussive blast of the bomb and was stumbling around, not able to hear or see properly. The medics got him to sit on the lip of wadi and started treating him. All three soldiers were put on stretchers when the medics heard the CASEVAC choppers in the air. There is an irony to this, as evacuating wounded soldiers was the drill A Company practised earlier that day. At the time, no one stopped to think about it. It only seemed strange the next day.

The helicopter arrived from the Kandahar Airfield but landed on the wrong side of the wadi. The soldiers had to scramble down the ditch and back up again. Ford told the soldiers not to drop him, at the same time asking how the rest of the soldiers in his section were doing. No one answered him when he asked about Green.

Before the chopper left, Perry and Decaire were also ordered aboard. The two corporals briefly protested — they did not think their injuries were that serious, even though there was blood on their uniforms — but they complied.

It takes four minutes for the CASEVAC chopper to get back to the airfield. When it lands Ford is taken immediately into the operating room at the U.S. medical tent, known as Charlie Med. He stayed there for six hours.

Just like Stogran, Steve Borland became aware of what was happening at Tarnak Farm as though it were a dream. A boom — or something like a boom — heard while sleeping. It was a sergeant-major who came and woke him, told him what had happened. A training accident, KIAs and guys injured.

He rolled out of bed, got dressed, and ran to the command post. He saw Stogran standing over the radio console, looking tired and ashen-faced. Peter Dawe was talking on the radio to Joe Jasper, and even if he hadn't heard what the two men were saying, he would have known something bad had happened. You could see it in everyone's eyes.

As he stood there, General Wiercinski arrived, and the look in his eyes was the same. By then everyone in the command post knew a bomb had been dropped by an American pilot, but no one resented the American commander's presence. Soldiers had been killed that night, and the nationality didn't matter to the brigade commander. Those had been his guys out there, part of Task Force Rakkasan, and he was as ashen-faced and confused as anyone else.

As Borland stood in the back of the command post, wondering what Stogran would want him to do, he heard Jasper start to read off the zap numbers for the wounded soldiers. Zap numbers are the military ID numbers assigned to every soldier in Afghanistan. They are assigned for all sorts of practical and logistical reasons, but one of the reasons was exactly what was happening — so the identity of a wounded or dead soldier could be sent over the radio without his buddies finding out.

Borland listened to the zaps for the eight wounded soldiers, watching as Dawe wrote them down and gave them to someone to cross-reference with the nominal roll, so they could get the names. Then he asked Jasper for the priority-four zaps. There was a short gasp from everyone in the command post when Jasper read out not two, but four zap numbers.

After that the list was passed along to each soldier in the command post, people looking at the names, shaking their heads, and passing along the piece of paper. No one could figure out what Léger's name was doing on the paper. He was a stores-man.

BOSSMAN was back on the radio to Schmidt. "Need type bomb dropped, result, and type of SAFIRE," he says.

"Yeah, it was a single GBU 12 dropped. It was a direct hit on, uh, the artillery piece that was firing. Uh, as far as the SAFIRE, multiple rounds it looked like, uhh, MLRS," Schmidt answers, and then he asks Umbach: "What do you have on that?"

Umbach answers: "I'd say the same. It was, uh, sort of continuous fire and uh, it appeared to be, uh, leading us as we were, ah, flying by and then as we came back around."

The AWACS controller still wanted more information. "Did you get a top altitude on the SAFIRE?"

"Negative," says Umbach. "They, ah, they were burning out before here."

"I would estimate the top was approximately 10,000 feet," says Schmidt, then quickly adds, "and, uh, just to let you know we split in azimuth, sending 51 to the south and 52 sent to the northeast and, uh, one of the guns turned back around to the east, uh, firing at, uh 52, uh, as well."

"BOSSMAN copies," replies the AWACs controller. "Can we get a rough longitude?"

"Yeah, I did not take a mark at the time," says Schmidt.

The controller asks for the coordinates Schmidt originally gave him, but the pilot replies: "I do not have the, uh, proper coordinates for that, uh, BOSSMAN."

BOSSMAN tells the two pilots to proceed to their rendezvous with the fuel tanker. Before switching off the radio, Schmidt says to Umbach: "Standby for the microscope, huh?"

Umbach gave his second one-word answer of the day — "Yeah."

Most of A Company left Tarnak Farm in the middle of the night, Hackett didn't want his troops there when the sun came up. Especially the younger soldiers. He took them back to the Kandahar Airfield, leaving the range in charge of Joe Jasper, who, along with some other senior officers, continued the search for undetonated explosives and body parts.

When they got back to the airfield they gathered in the television tent, where the battalion's operations officer, Shane Schreiber, who had been in the command post, gave them the news. Most of the soldiers still didn't know what exactly has happened. They'd just been hearing rumours.

Schreiber tells them eight soldiers had been wounded, including Sergeant Lorne Ford, who was being operated on as he spoke. It's a bad wound. Then he takes a deep breath and gives them the rest of the news. Four soldiers are dead. He reads the names, then starts to cry.

The soldiers back at Tarnak Farm stay until the battalion chaplain comes out the next morning to administer last rites. After that they put the dead soldiers into body bags and load them into an ambulance for the drive back to the Charley Med, where autopsies were performed. While they waited for the chaplain, other soldiers arrived at the range. Captain James MacEachern from National Investigative Services (NIS) arrived. NIS was then in charge of the range.

An Explosives Ordnance Disposal unit (EOD) arrived as well. There were still unexploded claymore mines on the training ranges and the paramedics reported seeing some hand-grenades as well. An American Disaster Mortuary Affairs Response Team also arrived at Tarnak Farm. It is a strange twist of fate that one. The squad is only in Kandahar because four American soldiers were killed earlier in the week, while trying to blow up a cache of Taliban rockets. The morticians and forensic investigators were scheduled to leave Kandahar that morning.

The Canadians tell the Americans they can find body parts, uniform fragments, the remains of weapons, and bits of the GBU every place they find a glow stick. The Canadians had been putting glow sticks out most of the night. The Americans look up and down the wadi and across the desert, where hundreds of glow sticks are waiting for them.

CHAPTER NINETEEN

Ray Henault had called a press conference at National Defence Headquarters for midnight. Despite the late hour, dozens of reporters stood in front of him, waiting to hear what the chief of the defence staff had to say about a story that had been circulating around Ottawa for two hours. Quoting unnamed military sources, the *National Post* was reporting at least one Canadian soldier had been killed in Afghanistan, apparently by friendly fire.

Henault had been attending a dinner at American Ambassador Paul Cellucci's residence, when he received a phone call telling him what had happened at Tarnak Farm. Apologizing to Cellucci, who had yet to hear the news, Henault went to his office at National Defence Headquarters. Once there, he had an aide contact the defence minister, who was working at his nearby parliamentary office. Not told over the phone what had happened, only that it was urgent, Eggleton headed to NDHQ.

Henault briefed him on what had happened: KIAs, many soldiers injured, reports still coming in, although it looked like friendly fire. Eggleton phoned Prime Minister Chrétien, who was having dinner with his wife at Harrington Lake, the prime ministerial country home. Years later, Eggleton would remember this call as one of the most difficult he had to make in his political career, the prime minister shaken by the news, the two men talking for several minutes.

Shortly after speaking to Eggleton, Chrétien would receive a phone call from U.S. President Bush, who expressed his condolences. In the coming days, Chrétien would describe the phone call with the American president as "emotional," even though Bush would soon be criticized in Canada for not speaking publicly about the friendly fire mishap for three days.

Back at NDHQ, Eggleton started making a round of phone calls — Government House Leader Ralph Goodale, Deputy Prime Minister John

Manley, Foreign Affairs Minister Bill Graham — while Henault continued getting briefings on what had happened in Afghanistan. Shortly before 10:00 p.m. the two men were told about the *National Post* story. It was early enough in the evening for the nightly newscasts to pick it up and plans were quickly made to hold a news conference. By this time, Henault had been told the number of dead soldiers was actually four. For a long time he was thinking it had been only two, the number originally reported from the confusion of Tarnak Farm. Now he stared out at the room of reporters and began the press conference by telling them the story was worse than they suspected.

"I regret to inform you," he said, "that four Canadian soldiers were killed and eight injured, some very seriously, when an American F-16 fighter jet released one, possibly two, five hundred-pound bombs on troops of the battle group involved in a night firing exercise on a range fourteen to fifteen kilometres south of the Kandahar Airfield in Afghanistan."

An investigation into the tragedy would be conducted by Canadian and American authorities, he continued, adding that there are inherent dangers to military service, but the Canadian Forces and federal government remained committed to the mission in Afghanistan. When he had finished speaking he took questions, the first one being the pith and substance of every question that would be asked about Tarnak Farm for the next three months: did he have any idea how such an accident could have happened?

Henault explained that the Canadians had been on a recognized training range, conducting a live-fire exercise that had been practised by all the coalition troops in Kandahar, and that American pilots fly "very well-controlled routes, under very strict controls." Then he paused, as though perplexed, and the former fighter pilot said: "How this sort of thing can happen is a mystery to us. That is what the investigation will determine. I can't speculate on it at this point in time. All I can say is that without a doubt, there was a misidentification of the Canadians and what they were doing on the ground and that was obviously the cause of this accident."

* * *

Shortly after the press conference, the prime minister released a statement:

> My first thoughts on this sad news are, of course, with the families of our soldiers who have been killed or wounded.
>
> Better than any of us, they understand the risks that are an unavoidable aspect of military life. But no amount of awareness or preparation can every truly cushion such an awful blow.
>
> Mere words are of small solace at times like these. Yet it is my hope that some comfort may be found in the knowledge that those who have been taken were serving their country with valour and gallantry in a great struggle for justice and freedom. And that each and every Canadian is proud of the exemplary manner in which they did their duty.
>
> As to the circumstances of what appears to have been a terrible accident, clearly there are many questions that the families, and all Canadians, expect to be answered. President Bush called me tonight to offer the sincerest condolences of the American people to the Canadian families. He also pledged complete American co-operation with Canadian authorities, who will carry out a thorough and complete investigation.
>
> Aline joins me in extending our deepest sympathies to those who are grieving at this difficult hour and offer our prayers for the full recovery of the wounded.

Shortly before the press conference in Ottawa, a car pulled up in front of Marley Léger's house and parked in the shadows cast by a spruce tree. Sitting in her living room, Marley saw it arrive. There were two men in the backseat, although she could only see the one closest to her, a tall man with a fine, hard-chiseled face and close-cropped grey hair that stuck out slightly from beneath his military cap. The other man was smaller, as she saw when they got out of the car.

The men climbed the steps and rang the bell. Marley let the curtains fall and made her way to the door. She wished she had another choice; that she could walk away, into the kitchen perhaps, or to bed. Visits like these never brought good news. She opened the door and then pushed open the screen.

"Mrs. Léger?" asked the man she had seen from the window.

"Yes."

"Ma'am, I'm Brigadier-General Fenton from the Edmonton Garrison and this is Father Vardy. Sorry to bother you at this time of the night, but we need to talk to you. I'm afraid there's been …"

She was already backing away from the door, her hands rising to her mouth, not hearing all that the general said next, staring at the man next to him, the man with a clerical collar, whose sad, large eyes looked right at her, pityingly.

That night notifications were made throughout Edmonton. Ainsworth Dyer's fiancée, Jocelyn Van Sloten, would get a knock on her door after Henault's press conference, after the prime minister's statement, after the news had already been on the radio and television. She had been out for the evening and had convinced herself Ainsworth couldn't be one of the four, otherwise she would have already heard.

Jodi Carter, Nathan Smith's fiancée, was notified and immediately tried to contact his parents, although she couldn't. They were not at home. She tried other numbers back in Nova Scotia until she finally tracked down Nathan's sister, who explained her dad was still on a ship, due to come ashore the next day. Her mother was on her way to Halifax to meet him. It was the sister who broke the news to Nathan's dad, going to the ship to find him.

Ricky Green's fiancée, Miranda Boutilier, was also notified after the press conference, having gone to the Edmonton Garrison for news once she heard what had happened. Many other spouses were there as well, but the garrison was not giving out more information than what had already been released by the CDS and the prime minister. They would know more come morning, they said, come back then. Later that night, when Boutilier had returned to the apartment she shared with Green, she would hear a knock on her door. She too knew what had happened before she was actually told.

In Toronto, Ainsworth Dyer's father also got a knock on his apartment door in the middle of the night. When he answered, an army chaplain was standing there. Dyer tried to listen to the chaplain, but it was as though the man had just been submerged in water, his voice distorted and coming from a long ways away. Paul Dyer had raised his son from the time Ainsworth was six. He had separated from the boy's mother, Agatha Dawkins, and moved from Montreal to Toronto for a new beginning, although the Jamaican immigrant had found nothing but sporadic employment and a tough life in the social housing high-rises of Regent Park. His son — his tall, handsome, soldier son — had been the best part of his life. Now he was gone.

Ricky Green's mother would be the last to be notified. Doreen Young was hard to find because she was at her husband's cottage, where there was no radio or television. She was lying in bed early in the morning when there was a knock on the door. Both her and her husband thought that was strange, there were never unexpected knocks on this door. The cottage was too remote. The road in too rugged.

Her husband got out of bed, then came back five minutes later to say she had to get up — gave her a long embrace when she did, without saying anything at first, then finally saying: "There are people here who need to speak to you."

When Young walked out of the bedroom there were military officers standing there, a sight so unexpected she couldn't help but blink her eyes, rub them with the back of her hands, as though they might be gone when she looked again. When they told her what had happened she didn't believe it. Green is a common name, she argued. So is Richard. It can't be her son they are talking about, because she is a mother and she would know a thing like that, would feel it instinctively, intrinsically, there would be something hollow inside of her and she didn't feel that.

"You've made a mistake," she told the man with the clerical collar. "It's another soldier."

The chaplain held her steady, defiant stare and said, "Ma'am, we don't make mistakes like this."

She started crying, falling to her knees, the military officers looking away and waiting until she had finished, so they could start to explain what was going to happen next.

While the notifications were taking place in Canada, Harry Schmidt and Bill Umbach were being interrogated in Kuwait. The two pilots were met at the Jabbar Airfield by Colonel David Nichols, commander of the 332 Expeditionary Force, who told them what had happened: four Canadian soldiers dead, an unknown number wounded. He ordered their jets and recording equipment impounded then brought the pilots to the briefing room they had sat in twelve hours earlier.

Inside the room other officers were waiting, including a judge-advocate general officer who would monitor the debriefing. A tape recorder was turned on, and before beginning, Nichols read a statement the JAG officer had helped him prepare. He told the pilots he was investigating the alleged incident of April 17, in which the pilots were involved. Anything they said could be used against them in a trial or courts martial. Did they agree to answer some questions? Both pilots agreed.

They watched the videotape that Schmidt's plane had taken of the bomb being released over Tarnak Farm three times before Nichols formally began the interrogation. Schmidt was asked why he felt threatened. Again he answered that he thought Umbach was being targeted by surface-to-air fire, and that he was being targeted as well. Both pilots said there were unaware of any live-fire training missions going on in the Kandahar vicinity, and that the action on the ground did not look like combat. This was not two forces firing on each other. It looked like they were firing at the planes.

Twice during the interrogation the tape recorder was turned off to have another look at the video. Both times, when the recorder was turned back on, Nichols asked a lengthy question about why the ground fire looked like surface to air. During the interrogation, both Schmidt and Umbach would say they had asked the AWACS for information about possible friendlies in the area — more than once they had asked that — but the AWACS controlled didn't provide any information, just repeated the order to standby, until Schmidt felt he had to declare self-defence.

Near the end of the interrogation, Colonel Nichols offered his own comments on the incident, stating that there had been chronic problems with getting timely and accurate information to fighter pilots from Coalition Air Operations Centre. This had been a serious problem during Operation Anaconda. He had raised it himself, more than once. The interrogation ended with Nichols giving a last statement and complimenting the pilots on making a "very good defensive manoeuvre."

During the notifications, interrogations, press conferences, and press releases the bodies of Marc Léger, Ainsworth Dyer, Nathan Smith, and Richard Green were still lying on the sand at Tarnak Farm. They could not be moved until the EOD had finished clearing the range, the DARMT had completed its work, and a chaplain had driven out from the Kandahar Airfield to administer last rites.

When all this was done, the soldiers from A Company who had stayed at the range overnight placed the remains of the four dead soldiers in body bags. To the soldiers who had stayed, it was important that this be a company job, although it broke some rules. When the bodies arrived back at the airfield they were brought to Charley Med, where they would be stored in the American morgue.

Much of the 3rd Battalion had been up most of the night, and years later the soldiers would remember the bodies being brought back to the base in different ways, some not remembering it at all, others disagreeing on the time, or the vehicle that was used, although certainly it was an ambulance. Grief, sleep deprivation, some sort of survival gene kicking in that mentally averts eyes that are staring straight ahead, the confusion could be the result of anything.

Stogran would remember:

> I think it was an ambulance, and I think it went straight
> to Charley Med. Body bags were being lowered, I have
> this vivid image of soldiers lowering body bags; so the
> bags must have been up high somehow. I'm not sure how
> that would have worked.

By the end of that day, all of us were running on no sleep, just leftover adrenaline. Much of what happened, from the time I was woken up and went to the command post, everything afterward, it's all a blur. I don't think I've had a day that moved so quickly, that was such an emotional roller coaster.

One moment I'm asleep, the next moment the sun is coming up two days later and I've got four dead paratroopers. That's the way April 17 was for me, the way it was for a lot of people.

CHAPTER TWENTY

On April 18th, 2002, a time before Facebook, Twitter, media apps, and smart phones, most of Canada learned about the deaths at Tarnak Farm at the same time. It was on the front page of their newspaper when they awoke. On the morning radio newscasts when they drove to work. The deaths of the four soldiers were a sudden mass shock, not unlike the terrorist attacks in New York City had been seven months earlier.

The passage of ten years makes it difficult to recall what that morning was like, how the country reacted to the first deaths of Canadian soldiers in a combat zone since the Korean War. Logically, Canadians knew their soldiers were on a combat mission again, after generations of peacekeeping, but it had been abstract, something unregistered and removed. That the deaths were the result of friendly fire only added to the shock, the incredulity and sense that overnight something had fundamentally changed.

By the end of the day a special website set up by the Department of National Defence, where people could post their condolences, was at risk of crashing. (A private website, started by an Edmonton businessman, soon had 80,000 postings.) Editorial departments at newspapers across the country were flooded with letters, many expressing outrage that Canadians had died at the hands of American pilots, saying the country should pull out of Afghanistan. The vast majority, however, were short expressions of sorrow, thanking the soldiers for what some called their ultimate sacrifice, what others called their patriotism.

In the House of Commons, while some politicians tried to get political traction from the tragedy — Alexa McDonough and Conservative leader Joe Clark both criticized the deployment to Afghanistan, Clark saying it was time for hard questions, the NDP leader saying it was time the troops came home — most of the Parliamentarians saved the jockeying for later sessions.

"At times like these we grasp for words of comfort and consolation, but they are just words. They can never do justice to the pain and loss that is being felt this morning," said the prime minister. Acting opposition leader John Reynolds went so far as to read two verses of Flanders Fields, before crossing the floor of the Commons to shake Chrétien's hand.

"It should always be a great source of national pride," Reynolds told the House, "that we have amongst us young people who volunteer to join our Armed Forces willingly and knowing that any day, at any hour, any minute, they may be thrust into perilous situations."

The families of the dead soldiers were besieged with offers of help from neighbours, friends, strangers. Each was given a military attending officer — someone who would be by the families' side for days, if not weeks. The officers helped the families make funeral arrangements, talk to the media; some were sitting beside them months later, when Pat Stogran came to visit.

The country learned of the deaths on a Thursday and by the following Monday newspaper columnists and television commentators were finding it difficult to describe what was happening. Perhaps it was the lengthy break between combat missions, perhaps it was the pall of September 11, which was still fresh in many people's minds, the troubling sense that the world had changed in ways that were unknown, destiny now some drunken and capricious troublemaker, some leering god; whatever the root cause, more than one commentator observed that this outpouring of national grief had never been seen for Korea, and was rarely seen for the Second World War. You almost had to go back to the battles of Vimy Ridge, or the Somme — where most of the Newfoundland Regiment was killed in the first two hours of battle — to find anything similar.

What was happening was shown in obvious ways — editorial letters, website postings, Parliamentary speeches — and in other, more private ways. One of the latter was the front lawn of Marc Léger's parents, a front lawn tucked away on a crescent street in a suburb of Ottawa, where before April 17th you would never go unless you knew someone who lived there.

Within days of the tragedy the Légers were on their way to Trenton Air Base, to be there when the body of their son came home. When they returned to Stittsville the next day, in the rock garden on their front lawn they found four Canadian flags.

The flags had been placed there by children from a nearby public school. None of the children had ever met Marc Léger, or knew of him. They just knew a Canadian soldier had died in Afghanistan. His family lived in their neighbourhood. And they found that extraordinary.

Stories about the fallen soldiers — who they were, where they came from — were printed and broadcast for days. One of them was the story of King Marco and the Livno Valley.

In 2000, Marc Léger was deployed to Bosnia with the 3rd Battalion, where he patrolled a war-torn part of the country known as the Livno Valley, a former Serb enclave that was ethnically cleansed by the Croatian Army. When the Canadian soldiers arrived, the Serbs were just starting to return to their villages.

It wasn't much of a homecoming. The Serb homes had been destroyed. Their fields razed. Their cattle and wells poisoned. There weren't a lot of aid agencies working in the Livno Valley either. The reasons for that could be debated, although certainly the Serbs were portrayed by most Western media as the villains of the civil unrest in the Balkans through-out the nineties.

Léger would patrol the Livno Valley, see people trying to repair homes without building materials, tend fields with loam that looked like the ashes you find in cold firepits, and before long he started to think it was stupid, patrolling this area without offering some sort of help. At first he helped old men move rocks, or offered water to children. Before long he started to "borrow" stuff from the Canadian base and take it with him on patrol, scavenging skills he took with him when he deployed to Afghanistan eighteen months later.

He would distribute building materials to the men repairing houses; bring the company water truck to fill cooking pots and plastic containers, and food from the camp kitchen. He talked engineers from the battle group into joining him, so they could make suggestions on the best way to repair stone houses that were missing a few stones. The more Léger helped, the busier he became, as it wasn't long before the returnees contacted other villagers, to tell them the Livno Valley was safe again, and what's more, there was this big Canadian soldier who was helping them rebuild everything.

Annoyed there was such little humanitarian aid coming into the valley, Léger began harassing the local UNHCR officer (United National High Commissioner for Refugees), asking him why Livno Valley was being ignored. While on patrol Léger would stop any civilian aid vehicle and tell the people on the trucks there was a pressing need right here, they didn't need to be driving straight through. His badgering got results. Aid slowly began trickling into the area.

It couldn't keep up with the influx of returning villagers, however, and one day Léger was told he might get more money and aid for the region if the Livno Valley had some sort of local government, political leaders who could petition the UNHCR directly. Léger thought this was a smart idea, and soon arranged a "town hall" meeting of the Livno Valley returnees. He explained what had been suggested to him, and said the people needed a person to speak for them, someone who could deal directly with UNHCR. The people at the town hall meeting also saw the wisdom in such an idea. They chose Léger to be their spokesperson.

Léger explained he couldn't be their choice. It needed to be one of them. He gave a quick civics lesson, explaining how an election worked, how voting worked. None of the people in the valley had ever voted, but again there was much nodding of heads, many compliments given to Léger, for coming up with such a brilliant idea. They held a vote, and elected Léger their mayor.

Again, using a translator, he explained that wouldn't work either. A Bosnian village needed a Bosnian mayor. It was the way of the world. They had to try harder. So the people voted one more time, and elected a mayor. They then held a second vote, Léger watching what was going on and not understanding. When the vote was finished he asked the translator what had just happened.

"They have voted you their king," the man said.

Militaries around the world are legendary for their rules and protocols, their slew of acronym-inducing proper nouns and reams of red tape. The death of a soldier is certainly no exception.

As soon as zap numbers were cross-referenced to a nominal roll early on the morning of April 18th, the work of getting the bodies of the dead soldiers back to Canada began. As the deputy commanding officer of the 3rd Battalion, Steve Borland was in charge of much of it. The first thing he had to do was establish a committee of adjustment, something done whenever a member of the Canadian Forces dies while on duty. The committee collects the personal effects, gets the paperwork in order.

Before the bodies of the dead soldiers had even returned to the Kandahar Airfield, their barracks boxes and rucksacks had been removed from their tents and quarantined. The committee of adjustment then sorted through the contents, separating personal belongings from what belonged to the military. The personal effects were itemized, catalogued, and placed into boxes, or back into the barracks boxes. The committee "sanitized" the personal belongings at the same time, which is military-speak for making sure nothing is sent back to Canada that will embarrass the soldier, or hurt his family.

Personal effects collected from a body are always sanitized. A blood-stained wallet will not be sent back to Canada. Nor will a watch that has been crushed and rendered useless, the time stopped at the moment of

April 19, 2002, a casket arrives at the Kandahar Airfield.

Corporal Lou Penney, Combat Camera

death. The doctors at Charley Med turned over the personal effects of the four soldiers and they were itemized, catalogued, and placed in boxes. While going through the personal effects of Ricky Green, the committee found the ring he had bought for his fiancée. Soldiers later told Borland that Green had carried the ring with him everywhere, always in his pocket, often showing it to the other soldiers in his section, always asking what they thought of it, even though the question had been asked and answered many times. "She'll love it, Ricky. You've done well."

After all the personal effects had been collected, the committee of adjustment turned the boxes and barracks boxes over to Wayne Green for storage. Given the mish-mash nature of the Canadian camp, the personal effects had to be stored in the open, until Green finally ordered tarps be placed over them.

Bank accounts needed to be closed. Death certificates collected from the American doctors. Cold-storage metal caskets had to be requisitioned, along with four Canadian flags. Borland also had to organize the send-off of the bodies, assigning positions on the Kandahar runway to the infantry soldiers of the 3rd Battalion, the Lord Strathcona's Horsemen, the engineers — everyone in the battle group — for the parade of bodies to the plane that would airlift them back to Canada. He also had to assign positions to the Americans, who had asked to be there.

When the parade was organized, chalks were assigned to the soldiers who would accompany the caskets back to Canada. Each fallen soldier was given an attending officer; someone of equal rank who would stay with the casket from the time it left Kandahar until it was interred in Canada. There was paperwork that needed to be completed for this as well.

Late on the morning of April 18th, Lorne Ford, René Paquette, Curtis Hollister, Richard Perry, Brian Decaire, and Norman Link had been flown to a U.S. Air Force Base in Ramstein, Germany. From there they were taken to an American medical hospital in Landstuhl.

Ford, Paquette, and Hollister were the most seriously injured. Ford had a badly damaged right eye and a left leg that doctors at Charley Med thought may have to be amputated. Paquette had internal injuries: ruptured eardrums, bruised lung, a concussion. Hollister also had a concussion, as well as burns on his face and neck. The remaining three soldiers had shrapnel wounds. The other soldiers wounded at Tarnak Farm, Master-Corporal Stanley Clark and Corporal Shane Brennan, were treated for their injuries at Charley Med and stayed in Kandahar.

After the eight-hour flight to Germany, the soldiers were surprised to see Adrienne Clarkson come aboard. The governor general had been in London — dining with the queen ahead of a state funeral for Princess Margaret — when she was told about the bombing at Tarnak Farm. The British Royal Air Force had flown her to Germany so she could be there when the plane from Kandahar landed.

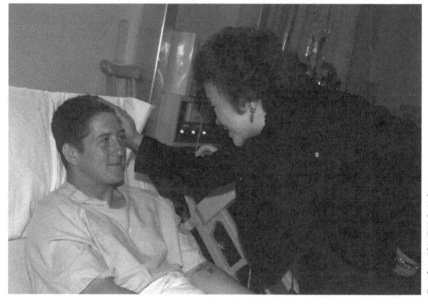

Governor General Adrienne Clarkson talks with Private Norm Link at Landstuhl Regional Medical Center, in Germany.

Master-Corporal Brian Walsh, Combat Camera

Her Excellency accompanied the soldiers to the hospital and stayed in Germany, spending much of her time in the hospital and startling René Paquette when he awoke from a drug-induced sleep and saw the face of Canada's governor general staring down at him. Before leaving the hospital that first night, Clarkson asked the soldiers if there was anything she could get them. Perry suggested beer. That night a case was delivered to their hospital room.

* * *

Reporters also arrived at the American military hospital. Some of the soldiers agreed to be interviewed. They gave their accounts of what happened at Tarnak Farm, although it was sketchy. They admitted they didn't really know what happened, just what they'd been told: an American fighter pilot dropped a bomb on them while they were doing a live-fire exercise. No one saw the plane, or the bomb. They were just in the wadi, or crawling out of it, and then there was a bright flash of light and a noise like nothing they had heard before.

At the end of his interview, Decaire told a reporter: "It's a shitty thing that happened and a dumb mistake by that pilot. I hope he's hurting now."

The comments were front-page news back in Canada, but were downplayed by Defence Minster Eggleton, who said:

> This is a time for sorrow, and reflection, this is not a time for blame.
>
> The investigation will occur in the fullness of time on all of these matters and will be appropriately dealt with through a board of inquiry established by both Canada and the U.S.
>
> We all know that in conflicts there are accidents. It happens throughout the wars, throughout the ages. If we do something in this particular inquiry to improve that record, I think we'll have made progress.

Interviewed in Kandahar, Stogran also downplayed Decaire's angry outburst. "We came here expecting a very dangerous mission," he said. "All we could do is mitigate the risk wherever we could, and go out and do the best job we can and not second-guess our fate."

The ramp ceremony in Kandahar was held early in the morning, the sun not yet out. Years later, Borland remembered how it looked, the troops assembling in the darkness, no light on the airfield except the spotlights in the detainee compound and the back ramp of the plane, which had already been lowered, red-and-green control-panel lights blinking inside.

The Canadian battle group had a little more than eight hundred troops. Except for the ones manning observation posts on the line, or doing other can't-leave duties, they were all there. The Americans had more troops, and except for those working duties that they also could not avoid, they were all there as well, all the assembled soldiers standing beneath regimental and company colours.

The caskets were driven onto the tarmac in the back of camouflaged trucks, then taken out and lined up in a row by the ramp doors of the C -17. The soldiers listened as General Wiercinski gave a short speech to his "brothers in arms," expressing his shock and sorrow at what an American pilot had done to them at Tarnak Farm. After that it was Stogran's turn, and from his pocket he pulled an email from Canada that he received the day after the bombing, that — as near as he can figure from doing the math on the time difference between Canada and Afghanistan — came at the exact moment Harry Schmidt was yelling "self-defence" and dropping a GBU-12 Pathway.

April 19, 2002, the caskets of Private Richard Green, Private Nathan Smith, Corporal Ainsworth Dyer, and Sergeant Marc Léger loaded on the place for the return home.

The email is from an old friend, who had read something in the Bible that made him think of Canadian soldiers in Afghanistan and the risks they were taking. The message had actually spooked Stogran when he received it, and as he stood in front of his troops he tried to keep his hands from shaking as he looked again at Psalm 139, written by David. He began to read:

> O Lord, you have searched me and you know me.
> You know when I sit and when I rise;
> You perceive my thoughts from afar.
> You discern my going out and my lying down;
> You are familiar with all my ways.
> Before a word is on my tongue
> You know it completely, O Lord.
> You hem me in — behind and before;
> You have laid your hand upon me.
> Such knowledge is too wonderful for me,
> too lofty for me to attain.
>
> Where can I go from your Spirit?
> Where can I flee from your presence?
> If I go up to the heavens, You are there,
> if I make my bed in the depths, You are there.
> If I rise on the wings of the dawn,
> if I settle on the far side of the sea,
> even there your hand will guide me,
> your right hand will hold me fast.
> If the darkness shall cover me,
> and the light around me become night',
> even the darkness is not dark to you;
> The night is as bright as the day,
> for darkness is as light to you.

Stogran then folded up the print out, walked up to each of the caskets, and although he had not planned it — he would remember it later as something that came over him, a spontaneous act that may have been spurred by the email, or lack of sleep, or grief looking for a short way to say goodbye — whatever the cause, he gave a sharp rap with his knuckles on each of the caskets, then yelled out the last words a parachutist hears before jumping from a plane, the words they hear from the jumpmaster who has checked the chute and cleared them for descent: "You're OK Jumper."

The plane touched down at the Trenton Air Base shortly before 11:00 a.m. on April 20th. Hundreds of people were gathered on the tarmac for the return of the four dead soldiers. In the crowd were Prime Minister Chrétien and his wife, Aline, Chief of the Defence Staff Ray Henault, and Defence Minister Art Eggleton, who stood next to Alice Léger, comforting the elderly woman as she broke down at the sight of the caskets coming off the plane.

The flag-draped caskets were carried to waiting hearses by eight pall-bearers, a lone bagpiper playing as the soldiers walked past a colour guard comprised of members of the Parachute Training Centre at the air base, all of whom were members of the Princess Patricia's Canadian Light Infantry. There were no speeches. This was not the time.

Sergeant Dennis J. Mah, Combat Camera

Minister of National Defence Art Eggleton (left) with Chief of Defence Staff General Ray Henault, on the tarmac at Trenton Air Base.

The hearses were escorted off the air base by Ontario Provincial Police cruisers, who then drove down Glen Miller Road and onto Highway 401, to make the trip to the coroner's office at the Centre for Forensic Sciences in Toronto. As the convoy made its way to Toronto, it passed thousands of people lined up on highway overpasses. The onlookers waved Canadian flags and saluted the hearses. The soldiers who were part of the convoy were surprised at the sight of the mourners. Unlike the ceremony back at the air base, this had not been in any military briefing booklet.

In the coming years this citizen's guard of honour would come out each time a soldier makes the journey from the Trenton Air Base to the coroner's office in Toronto. In 2007 the Ontario Ministry of Transportation designated the stretch of highway between Glen Miller Road and the Don Valley Parkway as the Highway of Heroes.

The soldiers who accompanied the bodies from Kandahar stayed at the coroner's office while autopsies were conducted. When the bodies were released, one stayed in Toronto, while the others travelled to Nova Scotia and Lancaster. The last leg of the journey home was about to begin.

At 8 Wing Trenton, Ontario, military pallbearers carry the remains of Sergeant Marc Léger past a Guard of Honour.

Sergeant Dennis J. Mah, Combat Camera

CHAPTER TWENTY-ONE

The next seven days were like a national week of mourning for Canada — four funerals, culminating in a public memorial service in Edmonton, originally planned for the Edmonton Garrison but quickly moved to Skyreach Centre, the then-home of the Edmonton Oilers (now Rexall Place), when it became obvious there was no building at the garrison that could hold the expected crowd.

Ainsworth Dyer's funeral was first. It was held at a Mormon church in Toronto. Governor General Adrienne Clarkson, Foreign Affairs Minister Bill Graham, and Ontario Premier Ernie Eves were in attendance, along with four hundred other people. At the beginning of the service, Dyer's casket was wheeled into the church, followed by soldiers carrying his maroon beret, his medals, and bayonet belt.

Corporal Jan Berube was the officer who had escorted Dyer's body back from Afghanistan. With his voice breaking, he said bringing Dyer home had been the greatest honour of his life. Dyer's sister, Carolyn, spoke of how her older brother had practically raised her, was always there to protect her, make her laugh, teach her that things were never as tough as they seemed, you could always improve on what had been given to you in life. Dyer's father — the man who had doted on Ainsworth, made his congregation prayer for "my baby" anytime the soldiers was deployed overseas, or went on a training exercise — sat in the front row wiping away tears, unable to focus on the casket of his son.

As would be the case for each funeral, a eulogy had been written by a soldier in the 3rd Battalion, back in Afghanistan. The one for Dyer is by Corporal Di Capua, who wrote:

> Being a light infantry soldier is a thankless job. It constantly requires you to overcome obstacles. Unlike a carpenter, mechanic, electrician, there is no physical

result of one's workmanship or accomplishments at the end of the day. Being a light infantry soldier requires toil and stubborn perseverance to overcome obstacles such as cold, wet weather, rugged mountainous terrain, mud, snow, driving wind or rain, fog both day and night always carrying a heavy load.

There is nothing comfortable about being a light infantry soldier. Most people have a difficult time to truly appreciate the sacrifices and endurance it takes to persevere through hardship when you're cold, hungry, thirsty, and lacking sleep. Nevertheless, it is the best time to see and discover who you really are. When the elements wear you down to a hypothermic or dehydrated state, your true character will come out. Ainsworth's character radiated like a warm, shining glow.

Ainsworth Dyer was twenty-four.

The funeral for Nathan Smith was held the next day in Dartmouth, Nova Scotia. It was a private family affair, one hundred mourners at St. Luke's Anglican Church. His fiancée, Jodi Carter, stood on the steps when it was over, holding the Canadian flag that had been draped over Smith's casket, breaking down when the casket passed and a three-rifle volley rang out, then pulled herself together and stood erect as a bugler played the Last Post.

The eulogy for Nathan Smith had been written by Corporal Kim Doerr, who said of his friend:

Nathan was a great soldier and a great person, and never was he happy with just a mediocre performance. He would spend his personal time reading military books and countless hours working out just so he could run faster and further, and carry an even heavier rucksack. Nathan never wanted to be called the best, or be the top, but in everything that he did, he was the best and the top.

The military was not Nathan's only love; his true love and most important thing in his life was his fiancée, Jodi, whom he loved and cared for more than anything else on earth. Nathan and I have been very close friends inside and outside of our jobs, and one thing that I will always remember is never once hearing him complain, or get angry at anything or anyone. He would simply flash a goofy smile and soldier on.

Nathan Lloyd Smith was twenty-six.

The funeral for Marc Léger was held the same day, in Lancaster, Ontario. Hundreds of people were at St. Joseph Roman Catholic Church for the funeral. Speakers were set up outside the church so the people who could not get inside could hear the service. The town's fairgrounds had been converted to a parking lot, every business in the village closed down for three hours, and a train that rumbled through Lancaster at the time of the service, a Via Rail train running between Montreal and Toronto, unfurled a Canadian flag and waved it from the engineer's car as it passed.

Jean Levac, Ottawa Citizen

Marley Léger holds her husband's maroon beret, and the flag that was draped over his casket, following his funeral.

Pallbearers carry the casket of Marc Léger into St. Joseph's Roman Catholic Church for his funeral in Lancaster, Ontario.

At the end of the service, Marley Léger addressed the mourners as though she were speaking to her dead husband, ending with the words: "I love you and will always love you. Until we meet again. Goodbye, my sweet love." The photo of her standing on the steps of the church as her husband's casket is wheeled out the front doors, ran on the front page of just about every newspaper in Canada the next day.

The eulogy was by Major Shane Schreiber, the former commander of Alpha Company, who, after telling the story of King Marco and the Livno Valley, said:

> I don't know what the Livno Valley looks like today. King Marco's empire may have returned to ruins, although I doubt that, as King Marco was as diligent in his succession as he was in his rule, something few rulers ever strive for or manage to achieve.
>
> I do know that for many, his compassion was truly and deeply heroic, and added to his already tall stature as a leader and soldier. For his work in the Livno Valley,

Sergeant Léger was deservingly awarded a Deputy Chief of Defence Staff Commendation last year. He didn't think that he had done anything that anyone else wouldn't have done, and that many hadn't already done.

What I find incredible about this story is that Sergeant Léger was not all that much different from every other trooper in my company. What I find even more surprising is how an institution as publicly maligned as the Canadian army can continue to consistently attract and retain guys like Marc Léger. As Canadian historian Jack Granatstein has said of another Canadian army at another time, it is probably a better army than the people of Canada know or deserve.

Marc Daniel Léger was twenty-nine.

Ricky Green was the last to be buried. His funeral was the following day, in Hubbards, Nova Scotia. The service also held in a church called St. Luke's, named after a saint from the Old Testament considered one of the four evangelists. More than two hundred people filled the pews of the small church, another hundred gathered in the basement listening on speakers. Canadian Forces padre Jack Barrett told the mourners: "We should not try to sanitize his death with clichés like 'you should be proud he died for his country.' There is no comfort in those words to a family who has lost one so dear."

Darrell Oake, The Daily News (Halifax)

Miranda Boutilier kisses the casket of her fiancé, Private Richard Green, during his funeral in Hubbards, Nova Scotia. On her hand is the engagement ring found on Green's body.

Miranda Boutilier did not speak during the service, although her sobs could be heard throughout, an unsettling counterpoint to the hymns and eulogies. She embraced the casket before it was wheeled out of the church, so bereft she had to be pulled away. Photographers caught the image and in a photo that ran in newspapers the following day, an engagement ring could be clearly seen on the wedding finger of her left hand.

Green's eulogy was by Sergeant Craig Reid, who wrote:

> Rick made the most of things and always performed his job to the best of his abilities. He took pride in his military accomplishments, but perhaps his proudest moment was when he bought an engagement ring for his return to Canada. While showing off the ring, his joy was something that affected all around him, and personified the best qualities in him. It was an honour to serve with Rick, pass on knowledge and experience to him, and see him blossom as a soldier and man.
>
> His pride in being a paratrooper, wearing the uniform and serving the country, was an inspiration to all who knew him. Although words cannot express the grief felt, we are all proud of him and he will never be forgotten. Rick believed in the importance of our goal, and as he did our country proud through his service, those of us remaining will carry on and strive to meet his example. As Rick watches from above, we will continue to do Canada proud, just the way he did.

Richard Anthony Green was twenty-one.

That Sunday, ten days after the bombing of Tarnak Farm, a memorial service was held in Edmonton. More than 16,000 people were there, including Prime Minister Jean Chrétien, Governor General Adrienne Clarkson, and United States Army Chief of Staff Eric Shinseki.

As coincidence would have it, half an hour before the memorial service began the Department of National Defence issued a press release saying another soldier had been wounded in Kandahar. The release said the soldier had been injured that day when the Humvee he was riding in drove over an anti-personnel mine. The soldier received minor injuries.

There was no reference to the wounded soldier in the two-and-a-half-hour service that followed. Former-Chief of the Defence Staff John de Chastelain spoke of the history of the Princess Patricia's Canadian Light Infantry, the regiment of which he was the colonel. He spoke of Kapyong and Frezenberg, Vimy and the Medak Pocket, archive photos of trenches in Northern France and hillsides in Croatia flashing on a large screen as he talked.

Governor General Clarkson gave a tribute that was interrupted numerous times by loud applause, the former journalist using the words of William Shakespeare, Greek statesman Pericles, and the Book of Isaiah to explain the loss of the four soldiers. She had addressed the battle group before it left for Afghanistan, she reminded those in the Skyreach Centre, and had told the soldiers "they would gain strength as they went, that vulnerability and strength are complementary, not opposites."

Lieutenant-Colonel Pat Stogran speaking to reporters in Kanadahar, following the deaths of the first Canadian combat soldiers in nearly fifty years.

She continued, "The men we honour today — Marc Léger, Ainsworth Dyer, Nathan Smith and Richard Green — were vulnerable as they were strong, even in death."

Prime Minister Chrétien also spoke, as did Chief of the Defence Staff Henault, although after Clarkson's poetic tribute to the fallen soldiers, the most moving memorial came from Pat Stogran, not so much for what he said, but the way in which the message was conveyed — by video, from Kandahar.

Dressed in his camouflage uniform and looking like a man who hadn't slept in days, Stogran spoke of the outpouring of support and sorrow that had swept across Canada in the past ten days, and what it had meant to his soldiers. He said everyone in the battle group remained committed to the mission in Afghanistan and would see it through, as the four fallen soldiers would have wanted them to do.

For many people in the Skyreach Centre, watching Stogran's video was like watching a moon landing, or a Soviet-era hockey game, a glimpse at a place not normally seen, at people not normally encountered. A Canadian soldier on a combat mission. In a place called Kandahar. It was fascinating. It was otherworldly.

While he did not say it in his video, earlier in the week Stogran had told reporters his troops were angry and bewildered by what had happened at Tarnak Farm, by what the Afghan mission had suddenly become — a ramp ceremony on the airfield, good soldiers going home in caskets, the loss of expected outcomes. He was asked his opinion on what had happened and, after stumbling through an answer, finally said this was not the time to try and make sense of it. For the soldiers who were out at Tarnak Farm, for himself, for everyone in the battle group, it was going to take "tens year to sort out."

Those words were not part of the service at Skyreach Centre, nor the words of the DND press release. And thus the service truly was a memorial, a remembrance of things past, things concluded, bereft of prophecy, although that could, as the record shows, easily been included.

PART V
Redeploy

The end is where we start from.

— T.S. Elliott, *Four Quartets*

Even a successful war is a loss to most families.

— Edward Counsel, *Maxims*

Paul Dyer sat in the restaurant and said his church didn't approve of smoking or drinking, and because of this he had begun to question his faith. He said this as he ordered another beer, asking Stogran if he wanted one as well. Stogran said he did. When the beer came both men lit cigarettes and resumed talking.

"Did he suffer any?" asked Dyer.

"No. He probably didn't even know what happened."

"There was no warning?"

"None."

"How could that pilot have made such a mistake?"

"We're not sure. We'll know more when the report comes out."

Dyer nodded and took a sip of his beer while Stogran looked away. He told himself he wasn't lying to the man. The board of inquiries convened to look into what happened would have a lot of information to examine. Everyone on the range had been interviewed. He had been interviewed. People in Tampa, on the AWACS, the entire chain of command: everyone had been interviewed.

The investigators had also pored over audio tapes of the flight, maps of Tarnak Farm, flight records from the control tower at the Kandahar Airfield. There would be reams of documents supporting whatever conclusions the

Corporal Ainsworth Dyer.

two boards of inquiry would make. It would be a thorough, soup to nuts, military operation. Stogran had no doubts.

Yet at the end of the day, would it bring them any closer to understanding what happened? Say what you want, discover what you may, but this story was about one man, making one action. It couldn't be parsed down, or dissected, because it was elemental to begin with. Pushing a button. It didn't get much simpler. And how can you ever know, completely, what drives a man to do what he does? Knowledge is what you get when you break things down. When you're dealing with something singular, well, you could be in a heap of trouble.

"Did you know my boy well?"

Stogran looked back at Dyer. He was a slight man, greying hair, stooped shoulders; how could this be Ainsworth's father? That mountain of a soldier who stood a head taller than almost everyone else in his company — it was a mystery, though you could see the son in some of the father's mannerisms: the deferential nod of the head, the grace of the hands when they moved, the sad kindness in the eyes. Ainsworth had been one of the gentlest men Stogran had ever known.

"I was his CO. So we didn't socialize. But I knew him fairly well. I had a barbecue once, at my house, after one of the Mountain Man competitions. My daughter was quite taken with your son. They talked for a long time. She asked him how he could work that hard, how he could carry so much, didn't he ever want to quit? Your son told her he would put down his rucksack when Jesus was no longer on his back."

"The tattoo."

"Yes, the tattoo."

"He was proud of that. Myself, I would not have done it. I have faith, but I would not have done that."

A tattoo of Jesus covered most of Ainsworth Dyer's back. Not many people in the company knew that. It was not there for show, for comment, for persuasion. He put Jesus on his back, and it seemed enough that He was there, didn't matter if anyone else knew about it. Some soldiers, they could hardly wait to strip down in PT, show off the tats on their biceps, their chests, even their ankles and calves nowadays. Ainsworth had the biggest, most elaborate tattoo in the company, but only a handful of people knew about it.

"He threw me around once, in PT," Stogran said. "We were grappling. He picked me up and threw me like a sack of potatoes."

"He was strong my boy, yes."

"I don't think I've ever been thrown that easily."

"That was Ainsworth."

"I have a black belt."

"That's my boy."

They left the restaurant and drove to the Necropolis Cemetery, the air conditioning in the car a loud hum, the day humid and without wind. As they drove, Stogran realized his other three visits had been near water, the Atlantic Ocean for Green and Smith, the St. Lawrence River for Léger. Even though the days had been hot, there was a cool breeze when he had visited the gravesides. Here in Toronto, although he was not far from Lake Ontario, the heat was trapped. Nowhere to go. It clung to you like a flak jacket.

The car travelled up the Don Valley Parkway, passing the Dundas Street overpass, Gerrard Street, then cutting past Riverdale Park. That night he would catch a flight back to Edmonton and later that month he would turn over command of the 3rd Battalion. After the change-over ceremony at the Edmonton Garrison, this part of his life would be finished.

He wasn't sure how the battalion's deployment to Afghanistan would be remembered. No Canadian battalion commander had relieved him. He had turned the line over to the American 82nd airborne. What many people thought might be a nine-month deployment or longer when the 3rd Battalion left Edmonton the previous January, turned out to be six months. Afghanistan was more stable than the military analysts had predicted, al Qaeda was in full retreat. He had been told there was good intel on Osama bin Laden's location, and maybe the Americans wouldn't be there long either. That time the next year Operation Enduring Freedom might be over and people could get on with their lives.

Of course there would be new threats. September 11 had shown, just as Stogran had long argued, that terrorist organizations, international criminal gangs, were the new threats to nation states. And that threat was best confronted by well-trained infantry soldiers. Get as enamoured with technology as you wish, get right gobsmacked by the lethality of predator drones and stealth aircraft, but the world never changes as much as you think. Freedom is still dependent, by and large, on hard men willing to fix bayonets in the middle of the night. Churchill was right about that one.

A lot of people didn't want to hear that, of course, so Canada's Afghan mission would likely be forgotten. Or remembered as an anomaly. The first combat mission since the Korean War, although there were no real battles. Four soldiers killed, but not by the enemy. The hard work done by the battalion, like so much hard work done by Canadian soldiers since the Korean War, would be forgotten, or worse, never known.

The car drove under the gingerbread archway of the cemetery, past the crematorium, the graves of William Lyon Mackenzie and George Brown, and before long the two men were standing in front of a black marble tombstone with the insignia of the Princess Patricia Canadian Light Infantry. Beneath the insignia were the words: "Cpl Ainsworth Dyer, 3PPCLI, 29 July, 1977 – 17 April, 2002." At the bottom of the tombstone was the single word "Afghanistan."

"So my boy threw you around once?"

"Like a sack of old vegetables."

CHAPTER TWENTY-TWO

The 3rd Battalion Battle Group would deploy on two more operations before leaving Afghanistan. The first would be Operation TOR 11, a return to the Tora Bora region of Afghanistan where Osama bin Laden had fought coalition forces the previous November. Because bin Laden had not been heard from since that time, there was speculation he may have died in the battle. The 3rd Battalion was tasked with going into Tora Bora and making a cave-by-cave search for the remains of the al Qaeda leader.

As it had been for Operation Harpoon, the physical conditioning of the Canadian soldiers served them well in the mountains. American Special Forces had estimated it would take twenty-four hours for infantry soldiers to reach positions on the peaks of Tora Bora, where they would begin their search. The Canadian soldiers reached the peak in eight. On the mountains the soldiers found thirty fortified bunkers, most still containing food and munitions. They also found the graves of thirty of bin Laden's bodyguards. As for the al Qaeda leader, bin Laden had indeed managed to flee the battle of Tora Bora.

The second operation was Cherokee Sky, in Zabul Province, Afghanistan, where the governor was suspected of having strong ties to both al Qaeda and the Taliban. This was again a combat mission for the 3rd Battalion, which was tasked with going into Zabul and hunting down al Qaeda and Taliban soldiers. The governor was tipped to the operation, however, and when the soldiers arrived the rebels had already fled. They did force the governor to turn over thirty surface-to-air missiles found in his fort.

In late July 2002 the 3rd Battalion Battle Group began to leave the Kandahar Airfield. The battle group turned over the line to the American 82nd Airborne and soldiers boarded planes for a flight to Guam, where they would stay for three days of R&R before completing the return journey to Edmonton. Thanks to the Canadians, American jumpers inherited a much better base than what the 3rd Battalion was given when it arrived in Kandahar.

Canadian engineers had built watchtowers along the perimeter of the line and soldiers no longer needed to work out of First World War-era fox-holes. Mark Pennie had succeeded in figuring out the riddles of the plumbing system in the airport terminal, so there were functioning washrooms and showers. Thanks to Pennie, who would later be given a Meritorious Service Medal for his work in Afghanistan, the stench of burning shitcans would no longer be part of army life on the Kandahar Airfield.

The 82nd Airborne even had flagpoles on which to hoist their regimental and company colours, including a large one, a twenty-footer that Marc Léger had wrangled from an American stores-man after trading him some Canadian shepherd's pie MREs. Alpha Company's colours were lowered when it left Kandahar, carefully folded, and stowed away for the journey back to Canada.

The R&R stop on the way home was something new for the Canadian Forces. Stogran had long advocated for a "decompression break" after an overseas deployment, saying it was asking for trouble airlifting Canadian soldiers out of Kosovo, or Bosnia, or Rwanda — some of the world's deadliest combat zones — then expecting them to sit down for dinner later that same day with the kids and ask how school had gone.

A CH-47 "Chinook" prepares to land and pick up Canadian soldiers as part of TORII, in May 2002.

Staff Sergeant Jeremy T. Lock, U.S. Air Force

A decompression break is now standard operating procedure on all Canadian overseas deployments.

In Guam the soldiers stayed at a four-star resort with swim-up bars and room service, a discotheque on the main floor. They arrived to a hero's welcome, the streets around the hotel festooned with hand-drawn Canadian flags, the soldiers feted at every bar they entered, their money no good. The terrorist attacks in New York City were just ten months past and the citizens of Guam, an American territory, were appreciative of Canadian soldiers having gone to Afghanistan in search of al Qaeda. The story of finding the bodies of bin Laden's bodyguards in Tora Bora was cause for celebratory hugs and free drinks in every bar they walked into.

As welcoming a reception as they received in Guam, it was nothing compared to the one waiting for them back in Edmonton. For several days before the first group of soldiers arrived on July 28th, the city had been getting ready. The city's police officers had tied yellow ribbons to their cars. So had firefighters and paramedics. Buses flashed WELCOME HOME TROOPS as their destination signs, whenever they were leaving or returning to the municipal garage. People tied yellow ribbons to trees and lampposts along the route from the Edmonton International Airport to the garrison. Businesses changed their advertising signs to read: WELCOME HOME, or WE LOVE YOU.

When the first troops arrived at the airport there were two pipers there to greet them, playing "Scotland the Brave." Then buses took them to the garrison, where hundreds of people were waiting for them, all gathered in the hangar where they had been told, six months earlier, that they were going on a combat mission to Afghanistan.

Under a large Operation Apollo banner that hung from the highest rafter of the hangar, the soldiers were reunited with their families, news photographers catching them in clinches as tight as any you'd see in the fifteenth round of a heavy-weight boxing match. They snapped photos of small children running toward soldiers crouched in camouflage gear with arms spread wide, no one knowing at the time how common such photos would soon become in Canada. The second wave of soldiers arrived two days later, and on August 9th the city of Edmonton held a parade.

After that everyone went home to put Afghanistan behind them.

* * *

It didn't work out that way. The following year Canada would return to Afghanistan, first to Kabul, then to Kandahar. Many of the soldiers who were part of Operation Apollo would end up making several return trips to Afghanistan, although 2002 would be the only year the city would have a parade for them.

How a one-time deployment with the American 101st Airborne tuned into a nearly decade-long military mission has been the subject of books, countless newspaper stories, and much heated political debate. The precise political and military machinations may never be known, although the public record is this:

In August 2003 Canadian soldiers were again deployed to Afghanistan, this time as part of a multinational International Security Assistance Force (ISAF). This Operation was dubbed Operation Athena, and the soldiers came from the Royal Canadian Regiment in Petawawa, Ontario. Operation Athena was different from Operation Apollo. The soldiers were not tasked to hunt down al Qaeda or Taliban forces. They were there to provide security and help rebuild the civilian infrastructure in Kabul.

Despite the mission parameters, the first two Canadian soldiers to be killed by the enemy fell in October of that year — Corporal Robbie Beerenfenger and Sergeant Robert Short. The soldiers died when their Jeep hit an improvised explosive device while on patrol outside the city. (Perhaps in a sign of what was to come, the soldiers had been diverted off their patrol path by a large boulder, forced to detour right over the IED. It was a deadly, carefully orchestrated ambush. The boulder was later moved to Kandahar, to serve as the base for a memorial to fallen Canadian soldiers.)

Canadian soldiers would stay in Kabul for the next two years. In that time the Canadian government committed $250 million in aid to the country, including $5 million to support the 2004 Afghan election that saw former Northern Alliance leader Hamid Karzai come to power.

In February 2006, saying the mission in Kabul had been successful in establishing democracy in Afghanistan, the Canadian government sent soldiers back to Kandahar as part of Operation Archer. This was also a combat mission, again with the Americans, although that would change later the same year when command for the Kandahar region would be transferred to the ISAF.

The original plan had been to withdraw Canadian troops after Kabul, but when Parliament voted in favor of extending the mission by two years, and returning to Kandahar, it was like being a passenger in a car that just hit a long, drawn-out, banked curve. You were going to the end of the curve. And when you got there, you would be headed in a different direction.

In the spring of 2006 Taliban forces began a major offensive against military targets around Kandahar. By early summer six Canadian soldiers had been killed and rebel forces were massing throughout Kandahar and Helmand Province. In June coalition forces launched Operation Mountain Thrust, the largest military operation since the start of the Afghan War, with 2,200 Canadian soldiers, an equal number of U.S. soldiers, 3,300 British troops, and 3,500 Afghan soldiers.

The rebel forces took huge casualties during June and July, but did not retreat. The rebels briefly captured two districts in Helmand, before coalition forces seized them again a few days later. The size and sophistication of the rebel attacks took the Canadian soldiers and every coalition commander by surprise. No one had thought the Taliban was capable of such a prolonged offensive. Suddenly, after having already committed to a two-year deployment, Canada was at war.

Throughout the summer of 2006 Canadian soldiers — the 1st Battalion Battle Group of the Princess Patricia's at first, then a battle group from the Royal Canadian Regiment — fought daily battles with rebel forces. By September the Canadian Forces sent in a squadron of tanks and another five hundred soldiers to bolster the battle group. The fighting would continue for another two years at a pitched level, with some respite during the winter, but then the spring offensives would begin. Canadian soldiers fought in places — Panjwaii, Zhari — that would soon conjure images in their minds not that dissimilar from what Kapyong and Ortona conjured in the minds of veterans from previous generations.

On March 13, 2008, Parliament voted to extend the Canadian deployment for another three years; that spring there was another rebel offensive. It was not until the American troop surge of 2010 that there were signs of the rebel forces weakening, of that long banked curve starting to straighten.

By then nearly 150 Canadian soldiers had been killed since deploying back to Kandahar. Despite the ferocious fighting over four years, many had still died by way of IED or suicide attacks. The patrols around Kandahar and in the Panjwaii district were often as deadly as any of the seek-and-destroy combat missions. The futility of such deaths was not lost on the Canadian government, which began banning media from ramp ceremonies at the Trenton Air Base soon after the return to Kandahar.

Canadian combat operations in Afghanistan would come to an end in July 2011, the date Parliament had agreed to in 2008, but in December 2010, without a Parliamentary vote, the federal government extended the deployment in Afghanistan for another three years. The Canadians moved back to Kabul to begin training Afghan soldiers and police officers, a NATO-led mission. As of this writing there are approximately 950 Canadian soldiers in Kabul. The first soldiers to deploy on the new mission were members of the 3rd Battalion, Princess Patricia's Canadian Light Infantry.

Art Eggleton and Ray Henault would travel two very different paths in the years following Canada's first deployment to Afghanistan. Given the ying-yang, magnetic-pole difference in their personalities — Eggleton the gregarious, spotlight-loving politician; Henault the reserved, almost bookish-looking air force general — this should come as no surprise.

With the commencement of Operation Apollo, Eggleton became a political lightning rod in the House of Commons. He was criticized for sending sailors into a combat theatre without chemical-hazard weapons, then for sending soldiers into the Afghan desert with forest camouflage uniforms. The stand-up-stand-down this-time-I-really-mean-it waffling in the autumn of 2001 was also an embarrassment. The serious political body blows, however, started landing in January 2002, with news that JTF2 troops had been turning over al Qaeda and Taliban prisoners to American Marines.

This was an issue because the Americans did not consider the prisoners to be military combatants. Thus they were not POWs and did not have the protection of the Geneva Conventions. When first asked about the allegations in the House of Commons, Eggleton denied knowing anything about it. Then he admitted prisoners had indeed been turned over to the Americans. Then evidence came to light that the minister might have known all along that Canadian soldiers were turning prisoners over to the Americans. The flip-flop led to allegations he had deliberately misled the House.

In May of that year there were reports Eggleton had given an untendered $35,000 contract to his girlfriend, to study stress and other health-related issues on soldiers. In a cabinet shuffle later that month, he was unceremoniously dropped as defence minister. He was not even given a junior posting. Prime Minister Chrétien relegated him to the government's back benches. It was the first time since being elected to Parliament in 1993 that the former-mayor of Toronto did not have a cabinet post.

He did not run in the general election of 2004, and the following year Paul Martin appointed him to the Senate. His Senate office is directly across the street from the Centre Block of the Parliament Building, an almost barren office by political standards — only a handful of framed photographs showing the senator with famous people (Bill Clinton, Paul Martin), a downright miserly collection of editorial cartoons (one of the few shows Eggleton in a bubble bath, playing with toy battleships). It is as though he has just moved into the office, or is just leaving.

On a warm autumn morning in 2011 he was interviewed while sitting at a coffee table in the corner of that office, nothing on the table except a steno pad and a tape recorder. He was asked for his assessment on the nearly ten-year Afghanistan mission. This is what he had to say:

> It started with September 11. Of course, it's been so long you lose sight of where it began, but by September 12 we knew about al Qaeda and we knew about Afghanistan. We were examining our military options — how would we support the United States, what would Canada's role be, those were the decisions we needed to make right away. We had to be ready to move. The Americans were going to go into Afghanistan. We knew that. So how could we support our greatest ally?

… We could have gone in with the U.K., on a non-combat mission. I had meetings with the U.K. defence minister. But the U.K. wanted us to contribute bits and pieces to their deployment. A medic here, a support officer there. It seemed they wanted to keep the focus on European involvement as well, wanted a European mission. I'm not sure why.

Problem with the U.K. offer was we wanted to make a more formidable contribution to the effort than what they were offering. Backfilling in the Balkans was an option we considered for a while, to free up American troops so they could deploy to Afghanistan, but then that idea was discarded. I think we made the final decision to go to Kandahar the day before we made the announcement. The Americans had asked us to go, they needed a quick reply, and we agreed. I never used the word *war*, by the way. I was quite adverse to using it. Bush used it.

… I think we were well prepared, by the way. There was a lot of exaggeration at the time. The desert camouflage for instance. Most of our guys were in the mountains. And we didn't lose any guys, except for that incident, what they called the friendly fire. We wouldn't have sent any troops if we thought they weren't prepared. And people tend to forget, with Article Five, we had to do something.

We had spent many years peacekeeping, of course, so this was new for us. The troops wanted to do it. I suppose we wanted to show we could do it as well.

… I keep coming back to Article Five, because I think that's largely forgotten today, but that was unprecedented. That was a Cold War clause nobody thought would ever be used, and then it was. If there had been no Article Five, maybe there would have been no deployment. No Afghan mission at all. But when Article Five was invoked, doing nothing was not an option.

Today, I don't know whether the mission was worth it. There have been some steps forward, and a lot of steps backward. Al Qaeda has moved around. The power and might of the United States military hasn't been enough.

Afghanistan is just a failed state. I thought we would be out of there fast. It was the return that was the problem.

As for Ray Henault, he continued his steadily ascending career path. Never a misstep, never a wrong turn.

In November 2004 the former fighter pilot was voted the next chairman of NATO's Military Committee. He assumed the position the following June, stepping down as Canada's chief of the defence staff. He would stay in Brussels for three years before retiring and returning to Canada, where he now does consulting work for the Conference of Defence Associations.

Here is his take on the Afghan Mission, and the friendly fire incident at Tarnak Farm:

The former defence minister is right, it all started with September 11, and you do lose sight of that sometimes. I was in Bulgaria on September 11, on a military chiefs of staff tour. I had taken over as CDS on the 28th of June. I was at a reception, it was four o'clock in the afternoon, nine in the morning back in New York, and the cellphones in the room started going off. We carried on with the reception, but then fifteen minutes later all the phones went off again.

We left Bulgaria that night, took a military flight to Brussels, where the next morning the NATO ambassadors voted to invoke Article Five, if it turned out this was an outside attack. It was unprecedented. It showed how grave the situation was.

We put our units on short notice to move and began exploring our military options. What aid the U.S. might need. We all felt it was important to show solidarity with our strongest ally. 3PPCLI became a factor right away. That was our Immediate Reaction Force.

This was new for us, of course. A new undertaking in terms of what it represented. We had not been on a deliberate combat mission in quite some time. It took everything we had to get that one battle group ready for a six-month deployment, then we had to take them home for an operational pause. But the thinking at the time, I remember it being that we were making a long-term commitment to fight terrorists. I never thought it would be just that one deployment. The government's position was that we needed to make a meaningful contribution to the international campaign against terrorism.

Still, it was very fluid there for a while, things were going up and down like a yo-yo. It could have easily been a different operational scenario. It all happened very quickly. It came from Tampa. The U.S. was very anxious to have a trusted ally, and we were ready to help. So ultimately, it was Kandahar.

… On the night of the friendly fire, I was getting ready to go to the U.S. ambassador's for dinner. Over the course of the night, as I started getting phone calls, it became clear that something serious had happened, and I had to leave. I held a press conference that night.

The outpouring of grief, it started that first night, it was immediate. On that night, people recognized that this was really a combat mission. Began to realize what we were getting involved in Afghanistan. It was a sea change for the country. The outpouring of grief, in Edmonton, across the country, it was amazing, like nothing I had seen before.

Today, I think that was a very important moment in our history. It changed the level of support for our military. I think people are very proud of the Canadian military today. They recognize the dangers that were in Afghanistan, that Canada pulled its weight in that country. It is a difficult thing for Canadians to buy into combat, but I think that happened after the friendly fire.

As for the troops, [the Afghanistan mission] has sharpened their skills. They have earned huge respect in international circles. They can be relied on, no matter how difficult it gets. It was that way in the world wars. It's that way again. The troops are proud again of what they do. That is such a change from the years after Somalia.

It came with a price, of course. A lot of fallen soldiers, the injuries have been quite extensive as well. I'm not minimizing that. But is the military in a better place today? I think it is. I think that is the legacy of the friendly fire.

CHAPTER TWENTY-THREE

Most of the soldiers wounded at Tarnak Farm are still with the Canadian army. Brett Perry is now a warrant officer. Sergeant Decaire, who used to train for Mountain Man competitions with Ainsworth Dyer, is a search and rescue instructor in Winnipeg. Curtis Hollister is also a warrant officer, with Western Area Training. Norman Link is still with the 3rd Battalion.

Shane Brennan left the military shortly after returning from Afghanistan and is a police officer in Edmonton. René Paquette left in 2007 to apprentice as an electrician.

As for Lorne Ford, he continued to amaze his doctors and fellow soldiers. The man who was supposed to die at Tarnak Farm, then, when he lived, was supposed to lose his leg, ended up competing in a Mountain Man competition at the Edmonton Garrison a few years later. Ford did lose his right eye, and was assigned administrative duties for many years at the garrison while undergoing extensive rehabilitation on his leg, but he eventually reached his goal of being declared fit once again for active service. In autumn of 2011 he deployed with the 3rd Battalion back to Afghanistan.

The soldiers in the Canadian command post on April 17, 2002, have also fared well, for the most part, since that night. Peter Dawe, the battle group's operations officer, rose quickly through the ranks and in 2009, after getting promoted to lieutenant-colonel, got Pat Stogran's old job, given command of the 3rd Battalion, Princess Patricia's Canadian Light Infantry. In March 2011 he was promoted again, this time to colonel, and returned to Afghanistan as deputy commander, Canadian contribution, NATO training mission, Afghanistan.

Major Daryl Mills, the adjutant for the 2002 battle group, was promoted to lieutenant-colonel shortly after returning to Canada. He went on to become one of the few Canadian soldiers to serve in Iraq, part of an exchange program between the Patricia's and the American Army's 3rd Infantry Division. He was in Iraq for four years, eventually becoming deputy chief of staff for the 3rd division. When he returned to Canada he was awarded the Meritorious Service Cross and appointed commander of the Land Force Central Area Training Centre in Meaford, Ontario. He is currently posted to National Defence Headquarters in Ottawa.

Steve Borland would also be decorated following the deployment to Afghanistan, awarded an American Bronze Star in 2003, along with Pat Stogran and several other members of the 3rd Battalion Battle Group. In 2005 he was promoted to lieutenant-colonel and returned to Afghanistan as part of the United Nation's Provincial Reconstruction Team. This is where the paths of the soldiers in the command post start to fork and go in different directions.

To this day he's not sure why he did it, but on his way home from the airport after that second deployment to Afghanistan, Borland stopped at an Alberta Liquor Control Board store, where he bought a twenty-six-ounce bottle of Scotch. He began drinking in the parking lot, something he had never done before.

For the next eighteen months — even after he was promoted and posted to Land Force Western Area — Borland never stopped drinking. He drank every day — some days to take the edge off having been drunk the day before, other days because he hadn't been drunk the day before and missed it.

In the winter of 2007 he slipped on the ice outside his home and hurt his back. When he went to the base doctor the next day he said he had a high tolerance to Tylenol 3 and left the office with a prescription for Percocet. What a lovely drug that turned out to be; like drinking and stopping after the third drink, when you had a glow but weren't slurring your words.

When Borland went back to the base clinic the next week he told the doctor his back was still a mess and he was given another prescription. After that he started seeing other doctors. Telling them he'd just slipped on the ice on his walkway. His back was a son of a bitch. By the way, Tylenol 3 does nothing for me.

From time to time — like the time a base doctor diagnosed him with post traumatic stress disorder, Borland thought he had found the cause of his drinking — he wondered if he should stop, if things were spinning out of control. He'd think about it some, but then, when he got tired of thinking, he would take another drink, another Percocet, and the question would go away.

He started having blackouts at work. It happened once when he was taking part in a role-play exercise. He was supposed to be part of a pro-vincial reconstruction team, escorting members of the media around. He remembers starting the exercise, then everything went black, then he was screaming at a soldier playing the role of a news photographer, physically shaking the man and screaming at him for trying to take a picture of a dead soldier.

"Do you have any fucking idea what you've just done?" he heard himself yell. "Do you how his family is going to feel, when they see your fucking photo on the front-page?"

When he stopped yelling the man backed away and Borland's periph-eral vision kicked in, so the rest of the room came into focus. Everyone was staring at him, the man in charge of the role-play exercise actually tilting his head, as though he were looking at someone lying on a hospital gurney.

He remembers thinking: "All right, this can't be good."

Things came to a head in August 2007. Borland had gone to work that day with a Scotch bottle stuffed in his gym bag. At lunch he went to work out, spending his time in a washroom stall with the gym bag, leaving just enough time after his work out to have a shower and get cleaned up. Shortly before 4:00 p.m. his commanding officer walked into his office and closed the door.

"Steve," the colonel said, "I think you've been drinking today."

He didn't say anything after that. Didn't actually ask a question, which was unnerving and left Borland with only two options: tell the CO he was wrong, or confess. It happened so quickly Borland had the strange sensation of freefalling, of the physical world changing to something whispery and far away. He was almost grateful for the knot tightening in his stomach. At least that was tangible. Something real.

"You're right, sir. I have been drinking."

"Is there a bottle in this office?"

"In my gym bag."

"Get it."

Borland went to his gym bag and pulled out the bottle of Scotch, thinking, as he handed it over, that there was surprisingly little left. He had a sharp pang of regret when he realized he wouldn't get a chance to finish it.

"Anything else?"

"No, sir."

The CO turned and went out the office. He left the door open, though, and before his back had disappeared from view two MPs were walking in. *My God*, thought Borland, they had been stationed outside the office the entire time. This had been planned. There had never been an idle question asked of him, any doubt about how this was going to play out. The only fork in the road would have been the MPs searching to find the bottle, or Borland handing it over. His CO had come in with dead-aim certainty that his second-in-command was drunk.

"Colonel, you have to come with us," said one of the MPs, and Borland was led out of his office. Had to walk past open doors and cubicles, where people averted their eyes, tried to look busy, although there was no conversation, no one moving, an office that was not busy at all. Borland was taken by the MPs to the base medical clinic where he had a blood sample taken, then was driven home.

When he walked through his front door that night his wife had already heard the news. He didn't bother asking who had told her, whether it was an official call, or base gossip. He didn't think it made any difference. The recrimination would be the same.

Three days later he was sitting in a room at the Edgewood Addiction Treatment Centre in Nanaimo, and for the first time he began wondering why he started drinking after Afghanistan. He never drank like that after Croatia, or Bosnia, but after that second tour in Afghanistan, something changed.

He didn't think Afghanistan was the cause. Confirming that suspicion took three months in counselling. The counsellors told him there was rarely a single reason for a person tanking his life the way Borland had just done. After that he learned about the Big Book, the twelve steps, and how to take responsibility for what should rightfully stick to you, let everything else fall away.

"Some things just don't make sense, no matter how long you think about them," says Borland today. "It was like the friendly fire incident. Same damn thing."

* * *

If Steve Borland had the wildest ride after Operation Apollo, Pat Stogran had the most public. In August 2002 he handed over command of the 3rd Battalion to Lieutenant-Colonel Mike Beaudette. The rotation of command is a constant in military life, particularly in the army. Soldiers move from one position to another, one rank to the next, one Canadian Forces Base to another halfway across the country, then back again a few years later. There is a reason why outside National Defence Headquarters in Ottawa there is a bus billboard advertising the services of a moving company.

While the rotation of the 3rd Battalion command had been on the books for quite a while, Stogran gave up the job with regret. Commanding an infantry battalion had been the realization of — call it a dream, a desire, an aspiration, whatever you want — it was something he had wanted since Matagami, Quebec, curled up on a couch to watch the *Devil's Brigade*. That the battalion had been the first in Canada since 1953 to deploy on a combat mission — authorized to use deadly force against a declared enemy — only added to his sense of loss.

He was posted back to Ottawa that year and began working at National Defence Headquarters, then went to Joint Operations Group in Kingston. In 2004 he was promoted to colonel and in 2006 was seconded to the Pearson Peacekeeping Centre, a non-profit organization operating on the campus of Carleton University in Ottawa. The peacekeeping centre is funded by DND, the Department of Foreign Affairs, and the Canadian International Development Agency, its goal to promote peacekeeping and peace operations around the world. Stogran became the centre's vice president.

He loved the job. He gained a new respect for peacekeeping, which is sometimes maligned in military circles for its complicated rules of engagement, cumbersome bureaucracy, and an often poor record of actually keeping the peace. Stogran was never one of those soldiers who sneered at peacekeeping missions because they weren't combat missions. The man who lived through the siege of Goražde knew there was sometimes only a semantic distinction between peacekeeping and warfare, knew many Canadian soldiers had died in Bosnia and on other peacekeeping missions around the world. For the families of those soldiers, the fact that they didn't die in battle was no consolation. No earthly difference.

Still, he was taken by the passion and commitment of the people working at the peace centre. At the good work they were doing. And he enjoyed being back on a university campus, where he was often invited into classrooms as a guest lecturer. Although you could argue there was no connection, nothing more than happenstance, Stogran began pursuing other interests and hobbies around the same time, among them playing the guitar, something that would have caused howls of laughter from most of the soldiers who knew him.

In 2007, when his term at the peacekeeping centre was drawing to a close, a friend contacted him to ask if he had applied for a new position the Harper government had created. The position had been a campaign promise and when Stogran said no, he hadn't applied, the friend said he should get off his duff and fire in a resume. He would be perfect for the job of Veterans Ombudsman.

The Harper government thought so as well. On October 15, 2007, Stogran was appointed Canada's first Veterans Ombudsman. In hindsight — and given how his three-year term played out — you have to wonder what the Harper government was thinking. Perhaps a government known for its love of the military was taken with an application from the man who had commanded Canada's first combat troops since the Korean War. Perhaps the interviews — where Stogran's love of the army and his near-perfect, tough-commander mien would have been front and centre — won him the job. Perhaps it was just his resume, which is damn impressive.

Whatever the reason, it is still surprising that a government with a hard-earned reputation for controlling its message, consolidating power in the prime minister's office, expecting people to nod their heads when addressed, would appoint, to a highly public government post, the man who told Sir Michael Rose to take a jump.

Almost immediately upon taking up his new post, Stogran ran into problems. He told the mandarins running Veterans' Affairs Canada that he wanted to spend more time outside the office than inside it. "Why would you do such a thing?" he was asked. He needed to manage his office. Stogran said the job of ombudsman should be meeting veterans, not the people working in his office. In particular, he wanted to meet homeless vets; the people living in shelters, or on the streets, the ones with PTSD and other service-related illnesses.

We don't have such people, Stogran was told. That's an American problem.

Stogran left the office anyway, and went across the country talking to veterans. He instigated a campaign — Leave No One Behind, he called it — that made it formal policy in his office to go out and search for veterans needing help. It wasn't enough to sit in an office and wait for them to come.

He filed regular reports with bureaucrats at Veterans Affairs, Treasury Board, and the Privy Council, highlighting some of the issues and concerns veterans had raised with him. He would always receive a polite reply, thanking him for the information, a promise near the end of the letter to look into the matter. Yet nothing seemed to happen. His reports became more pointed, less polite, in time they even suggested that perhaps the bureaucrats weren't taking the office of Veterans Ombudsman seriously. This seemed to be confirmed in 2010 when he asked to be briefed by Veterans Affairs on the government's decision to compensate certain veterans who had been exposed to Agent Orange. In response, Stogran was mailed the news release the government department had issued.

Stogran became angry at the inaction, at the disdain he felt the bureaucrats were showing to veterans, to his office, and started telling the media as much. He accused Veterans Affairs of having a "penny-pinching insurance-company mentality" toward its clients. Went on to say, "Deputy ministers make more on average in one year than a person who loses two legs in Afghanistan can expect to be paid out for the rest of their life."

The bureaucrats tried to rein Stogran in, summoning him to meetings to say he was losing control of his office, wasn't doing the job properly. He was told, more than once, that being a high-ranking government official was different from being a soldier and he needed to learn how to "manage up." Needed to learn that damn quick. When Stogran asked what that phrase meant, he was told it basically meant keeping your bosses happy.

Stogran left the meetings wondering what the difference was between the bureaucratic phrase, "manage up," and the military phrase, "brown-nosing," but couldn't come up with the distinction.

What finally did him in was the New Veterans Charter, a sweeping overhaul by Veterans Affairs in the way it compensated wounded veterans.

The single biggest change was replacing the previous pension system, which paid wounded veterans a monthly amount for life, along with a survivor benefit, to a lump-sum disability award. Stogran felt this was short-changing veterans. He went so far as to call it "cruel-hearted" and spoke against it every opportunity he had.

In August 2010 Stogran was told his three-year appointment would not be renewed. He received the news in a letter, hand-delivered to his office, telling him his last day of work would be November 10th, one day before Remembrance Day. His response was to hold a press conference in Ottawa three days later, to announce his termination before the government did. He invited wounded veterans of the Afghanistan mission to share the podium with him, to talk about the New Veterans Charter.

After the press conference, veterans started a petition to keep Stogran as the ombudsman. Newspaper editorials criticized the federal government for the decision. Opposition politicians raised the issue in the House of Commons for several days, peppering Veterans Affairs Minister Jean-Pierre Blackburn with questions about Stogran's dismissal. The minister initially argued that the Order-in-Council that created the position of Veterans Ombudsman did not allow for a renewal of the appointment (the document did not say that), then said it was time for new blood.

None of it made any difference. On November 10th, Guy Parent became Canada's new Veterans Ombudsman and Pat Stogran went home, opened a consulting business, and resumed his guitar lessons. In the autumn of 2011 he started performing at open-mic sessions at folk clubs around Ottawa.

When asked for his thoughts on the Afghanistan mission he says:

> I think the original deployment was good. Alex Watson was rebuilding the schools, helping the local villages. We were winning the hearts and minds. That's the way you win a war. We should have done more of that, kept doing it. You know when we went back to Kandahar, and opened a Tim Hortons, that always blew me away. A Tim Hortons inside the wire? Fuck, we should have built it *outside* the wire. That might have done some good.

Instead we just retreated, hunkered down, and lost the hearts and minds.

The whole mission was wrong as soon as we went back to Kandahar. It was classic seek and destroy. It was almost identical to the American military strategy in Vietnam. People don't want to make that comparison, but it's there to be made. You never win a war with a seek-and-destroy deployment. You just add to a body count.

CHAPTER TWENTY-FOUR

Harry Schmidt and Bill Umbach never flew again for the Illinois Air National Guard. Relieved of their duties on April 18th, 2002, the pilots returned to the United States later that month. Canada and the United States formed military boards of inquiry to investigate what they had done. Each board concluded that, while there had been some communications breakdowns that night, the ultimate responsibility for the tragedy lay with the pilots, specifically Schmidt, whom the inquiries said had acted recklessly and in haste when he released the bomb.

The United States Air Force would go on to charge him with four counts of involuntary manslaughter and eight counts of assault. Umbach would be charged with four counts of aiding and abetting manslaughter and eight counts of aiding and abetting assault. If convicted of the charges, which the military considered "judicial charges," or criminal charges, both pilots would have been sent to Leavenworth Penitentiary.

U.S. Air Force Pilot Major William Umbach and his wife Marlene, enroute to the Article 32 hearing room at Barksdale Air Force Base (AFB), Louisiana.

Master-Sergeant Michael Kaplan, United States Air Force

As soon as the charges were laid, the case became a *cause célèbre* for many people in the United States. The war on terror was not yet a year old, Afghanistan and Iraq dominated the news, and criminal charges against fighter pilots was seen as an attack on the American military. On guardsmen, no less, people who, like Umbach, had put aside their civilian jobs to go overseas and fight for their country. Illinois Governor George Ryan held a fundraiser for the pilots. Lisa Schmidt appeared on television and was interviewed by *People* magazine. Schmidt's lawyer was high-profile Virginian Charles Gittens, who treated the charges against his client as an affront to American fighter pilots everywhere.

In January 2003 what is known as an Article 32 hearing was held at Barksdale Air Force Base in Louisiana. An Article 32 hearing is like a preliminary hearing in Canada, a hearing to determine if there is sufficient evidence to proceed with criminal charges. The Article 32 hearing lasted several days. At the end of the proceedings Schmidt and Umbach were asked if they had anything they wished to say. For people like Claire Léger, who had travelled to Louisiana to watch the hearing, this was the moment they had been waiting for. Neither man had spoken to the media, or testified during the hearing, they were still as much a mystery as in the days after the attack on Tarnak Farm, when no one even knew their names, when they went by the phrase "two American F-16 pilots."

Both pilots said they wished to address the hearing. Léger and other family members were watching by video hookup in a nearby room, along with soldiers from the 3rd Battalion Battle Group who had been called to testify. Bill Umbach spoke first.

> Sergeant Marc Léger, Corporal Ainsworth Dyer, Private Nathan Smith, Private Richard Green, Sergeant Lorne Ford, Master-Corporal Curtis Hollister, Master-Corporal Stanley Clarke, Corporal René Paquette, Corporal Brett Perry, Corporal Brian Decaire, Corporal Shane Brennan, Private Norman Link: I want to address your family and your friends.
>
> I fear that any words of mine will be weak because nothing that anyone can do can undo what happened.

I know that I will never understand the depth of your grief. I also know that those lost and injured were good men who loved their country and heard the call of duty to preserve freedom for all of us.

They have earned the highest praise: they were patriots, they were true heroes. Know that my family and I hold you all in our hearts. I pray that God will help you in your anguish ... not a day has passed that I have not thought of that night: in the sky, in the darkness, and all that has happened since. I deeply regret that this terrible accident has occurred.

Major Schmidt and I were doing our best to protect ourselves in a situation where we honestly believed we were under attack. I hope and pray for your understanding and forgiveness, and that all of the factors that contributed to this tragedy will be made known and fixed so that neither pilots nor their brave brothers-in-arms on the ground are ever in this situation again. If I could turn back time, I would. But since I cannot, I want you to know that I am truly sorry.

After Umbach had finished, Schmidt addressed the hearing. He is taller than Umbach, with a heavier build, and his voice never wavered. He had more of a presence in the hearing room, and people likely would have paid more attention for this reason alone. But this was the man who had called self-defence, rolled left, and, in the span of less than a minute, set in motion everything that led to this hearing room, and everything that would follow. Léger remembers it being an odd sensation, listening to him, as though everything in the physical word had been pared down to Harry Schmidt, speaking directly to her.

I would like to say first and foremost that I sincerely regret the accident that occurred. My heart goes out to the families of the men killed and injured in what can only be described as a tragic accident in "the fog of war."

The accident was truly unfortunate and I am sorry that it happened.

I was called upon to make a perfect decision in a rapidly unfolding combat environment. I had to make that decision with what I now know, with the acuity of 20/20 hindsight, was imperfect information.

My perception was that we had been ambushed, as we had been briefed that Taliban were expected to use ambush tactics in and around Kandahar. I believed that the projectiles posed a real and present danger to our flight and specifically to my flight lead.

While I was assigned to the 332 Aerospace Expeditionary Group, I was never alerted to the possibility of live-fire training being conducted in the war zone. Further, at no time prior to our mission on 17 April 2002 were we briefed of a live-fire exercise at Tarnak Farm or in the vicinity of Kandahar. Nor were we ever advised while airborne by the AWACS command and control platform, or any calls on the Guard frequency, that there was a live-fire exercise ongoing anywhere in the war zone. Because such an event in a combat area would have been so unusual and unexpected, information about such training would be the type of information we would note so that we could avoid it. This lack of information is the one link in the chain, which if corrected, would surely have avoided this accident.

I attempted to use warning shots to suppress the threat but I was denied by BOSSMAN. I finally communicated to BOSSMAN that I was engaging in self-defence because my flight lead was at risk of being shot down.

Finally, I would like to tell the families of Sergeant Léger, Corporal Dyer, Private Green, and Private Smith that I am deeply sorry for what happened. I will always regret what happened that night. Next, I apologize to each of the men I wounded. I think about the men who were killed and the men who were injured. As a family man myself with a wife and two young boys, I can only imagine how difficult it is for they and their families to grapple with the fact that these men volunteered to serve their country and were killed in a wartime accident. I sincerely want them to know that my heart goes out to them and that I am truly sorry for their loss.

Asked afterward what she had thought of the pilots' statements, Claire Léger said Umbach seemed sincere. As for Schmidt, she was surprised by how much time he had spent justifying his actions, blaming others for the tragedy. Other family members and soldiers expressed similar sentiments.

Jeff Mitchell, Reuters

U.S. Air Force pilot Major Harry Schmidt at his Article 32 hearing at Barksdale Air Force Base in Louisiana.

* * *

Schmidt has given few interviews in ten years, so there is only the public record to go by, but when you examine that record, Léger's observations at the Article 32 hearing seem prescient. The former Top Gun pilot, who had the world exactly where he wanted it before deploying as part of Operation Enduring Freedom, would continually blame others for what had happened, would fight long and hard against the charges against him, long after Umbach had given up, long after the battle seemed finished. He was like a man trying to reclaim a lost life.

Many would argue Schmidt got the best of all possible outcomes almost immediately, when in June 2003, six months after the Article 32 hearing, the United States Air Force dropped the criminal charges against him and Umbach, replacing them with a "non-judicial charge" of dereliction of duty. Umbach quickly agreed to accept a letter of reprimand, retired from the Illinois Air National Guard, and his charge was dropped.

Schmidt chose to fight the remaining charge. For the next year, Gittens fought a lengthy procedural fight over whether his client was receiving fair treatment by the United States Air Force, and again people rallied to the pilot's defence. The new Illinois governor, Rod Blagojevich, wrote a letter of support. Legal-defence fundraisers were held at military bases across the country. People in Springfield had T-shirts made, reading WE SUPPORT OUR PILOTS.

In the late spring of 2004, the United States Air Force Court of Appeals ruled against Gittens' motions and the case against Schmidt was allowed to proceed. On July 6th, 2004, Schmidt was convicted of dereliction of duty, docked a month's pay, and given a letter of reprimand. He was allowed to keep his job at the Illinois Air National Guard, although he could never fly again.

The letter of reprimand, written by Lieutenant-General Bruce Carlson, was scathing.

> You are hereby reprimanded. You flagrantly disregarded a direct order from the controlling agency, exercised a total lack of basic flight discipline over your aircraft, and blatantly ignored the applicable rules of engagement and special instructions. Your willful misconduct directly caused the most egregious consequences imaginable, the deaths of four coalition soldiers and injury to eight others. The victims of your callous misbehavior were from one of our staunch allies in Operation Enduring Freedom and were your comrades-in-arms.

You acted shamefully on 17 April 2002 over Tarnak Farm, Afghanistan, exhibiting arrogance and a lack of flight discipline. When your flight lead warned you to "make sure it's not friendlies" and the Airborne Warning and Control System aircraft controller directed you to "standby" and later to "hold fire," you should have marked the location with your targeting pod. Thereafter, if you believed, as you stated, you and your leader were threatened, you should have taken a series of evasive actions and remained at a safe distance to await further instructions from AWACS. Instead, you closed on the target and blatantly disobeyed the direction to "hold fire." Your failure to follow that order is inexcusable. I do not believe you acted in defense of Major Umbach or yourself. Your actions indicate that you used your self-defense declaration as a pretext to strike a target, which you rashly decided was an enemy firing position, and about which you had exhausted your patience in waiting for clearance from the Combined Air Operations Center to engage. You used the inherent right of self-defense as an excuse to wage your own war.

In your personal presentation before me on 1 July 2004, I was astounded that you portrayed yourself as a victim of the disciplinary process without expressing heartfelt remorse over the deaths and injuries you caused to the members of the Canadian Forces. In fact, you were obviously angry that the United States Air Force had dared to question your actions during the 17 April 2002 tragedy. Far from providing any defense for your actions, the written materials you presented to me at the hearing only served to illustrate the degree to which you lacked flight discipline as a wingman of COFFEE Flight on 17 April 2002.

Through your arrogance, you undermined one of the most sophisticated weapons systems in the world, consisting of the Combined Air Operations Center, the

Airborne Warning and Control System, and highly disciplined pilots, all of whom must work together in an integrated fashion to achieve combat goals. The United States Air Force is a major contributor to military victories over our nation's enemies because our pilots possess superior flight discipline. However, your actions on the night of 17 April 2002 demonstrate an astonishing lack of flight discipline. You were blessed with an aptitude for aviation, your nation provided you the best aviation training on the planet, and you acquired combat expertise in previous armed conflicts. However, by your gross poor judgment, you ignored your training and your duty to exercise flight discipline, and the result was tragic. I have no faith in your abilities to perform in a combat environment.

I am concerned about more than your poor airmanship, I am also greatly concerned about your officer-ship and judgment. Our Air Force core values stress "integrity first." Following the engagement in question, you lied about the reasons why you engaged the target after you were directed to hold fire and then you sought to blame others. You had the right to remain silent, but not the right to lie. In short, the final casualty of the engagement over Kandahar on 17 April 2002 was your integrity.

In Canada the discipline meted to Schmidt caused editorial writers and radio talk show hosts to say it was nothing more than a slap on the wrist — one month's pay for the death of four soldiers, the maiming of eight others. He didn't even lose his job, or rank. Considering he started with the possibility of twenty years in Leavenworth, it did seem a better-than-expected outcome.

Schmidt didn't see it that way. In 2006 he sued the Air Force, saying the reprimand letter had slandered him and never should have been publicly released. Although it would not be part of his legal action, he would also say the air force owed him money, claiming Gittens had worked out a deal that would see him continue to get paid a pilot's salary even though he would never fly again.

In September 2007 U.S. District Judge Jeanne Scott ruled in favour of the Air Force, saying: "The competing public interest in disclosure clearly outweighs Schmidt's privacy interest." The same year, after six years of being on administrative duties, Schmidt would retire from the Illinois Air National Guard.

Although Lisa Schmidt has been interviewed by the media several times, her husband only gave two interviews on what happened in the airspace over Tarnak Farm. One was to Canadian reporter Michael Friscolanti, for his 2005 book *Friendly Fire: The Untold Story of the U.S. Bombing That Killed Four Canadian Soldiers in Afghanistan.* Another was for a lengthy feature article in *Chicago Magazine*, published the same year. In the *Chicago Magazine* article, Schmidt continued to insist there were good reasons for dropping the bomb, and that he was not solely responsible for the deaths of the four soldiers, as the United States Air Force and two boards of inquiry had concluded. At various times in the magazine article Schmidt blames the tragedy on the chain of command, BOSSMAN, go pills, even William Umbach.

Schmidt repeats again the assertion he made at his Article 32 hearing, that he never would have dropped the bomb if he had been briefed about the live-fire exercise at Tarnak Farm. "The one thing we weren't told about was that there would be (friendly) live-fire exercises near Kandahar that night," the story quotes him as saying. "Nobody told us."

As for his role in what happened that night, "I was the wingman," he says. "I was not in charge of making decisions. I was 'Shut up, hang on and say yes, sir.' I was the lowest person on the totem pole. I was, in effect, along for the ride."

At several points in the article Schmidt's wife claims her family was also a victim that night. "My husband went to combat and has never come home," she says.

Schmidt makes similar claims. "As a parent and a husband, I can only imagine how devastating it must have been to lose a child or a spouse. I thought of how this has affected my own family. They were totally innocent in this, too, and yet they're intricately affected."

The article ends with Schmidt saying he has lost faith in the American military, and will advise his two boys, if they every express an interest in serving, against doing so. He doesn't want a repeat of what happened to him.

In September 2011 Harry Schmidt left a voicemail message for a reporter who'd been trying to contact him. On the same day the reporter was upbraided by Lisa Schmidt, who objected to him phoning the Schmidt home in Springfield, where the family still lives in the house by the golf course.

"Do not contact us again," she said. "We went through hell back then. We just want to put this behind us and get on with our lives."

Schmidt's phone message is polite, although halting, with many of the verbal mannerisms that were highlighted in the cockpit transcripts of April 17, 2002.

"This is Harry Schmidt," he says. "I am, uhhhh, just getting back to you. I understand you want to talk to me, about Afghanistan, and, uhhh, I appreciate the opportunity, but I'm going to respectfully decline at this time.

"I, uhhh, hope it goes well. Goodbye."

CHAPTER TWENTY-FIVE

Before leaving for Afghanistan in 2002, Marc Léger drove to a strip mall on 97th Street in northeast Edmonton. There is a Second Cup coffee shop there, a Bank of Montreal, a florist. The mall is about fifteen kilometres down 97th Street from the Edmonton Garrison.

The florist remembers him as a tall, good-looking young man who took his time picking out the floral bouquets. Serious, must have been there more than an hour, between picking out flowers and signing cards. He walked up and down the aisles, asking questions, picking out flowers while the florist waited behind the counter with the cards and a calendar.

"He said he was on his way to Afghanistan," she would say later. "He was buying flowers that he wanted delivered while he was overseas."

It was a cold day, and the windows of the shop had frosted over. Most of the time he was in there he was the only customer. Although the florist went to answer the phone from time to time, or cut flowers, it ended up seeming a lonely transaction.

"He was quite specific about what he wanted," she said. "And he wanted to write a note for each bouquet."

Léger must have driven from the base that morning, for he was wearing military greens. When she checked the date later it turned out to be the day before he deployed to Afghanistan. The visit to the florist seemed a strange prelude to what was to come: a quiet moment, neatly encapsulated, when Marc Léger chose his last words to his wife.

His first bouquet arrived on Valentine's Day, three days after he arrived in Afghanistan. It was a dozen long-stemmed red roses.

The second bouquet arrived shortly before his birthday, in March, a fine display of lilies and red orchids. The next bouquet arrived after his death, in late April. After that they kept coming.

There was no way of predicting when the flowers would arrive. Once a bouquet was delivered on a day when things had been relatively peaceful, when Marley had spent hours playing with Hunter, their dog. When the flowers arrived late in the day, it was as if Marc had walked through the door with them.

Two months after the 3rd Battalion returned to Edmonton, the final bouquet of flowers arrived. The short note read: "Always thinking of you. Love Marc."

Marley Léger has that note tucked away. She keeps it with some medals she was given after Marc's death. She plans on showing them to her daughters one day.

For several years after April 17, 2002, Marley figures she was running on grief and adrenaline and not much else. Every act she made was one of remembrance. Every gesture one of grief. She set up a memorial fund in Léger's name and used the money to fly to the Livno Valley, where King Marco once reigned, to help build a community centre. Later, she helped pay for a new roof on a Livno church.

She went to Rideau Hall. Spoke to the media whenever Harry Schmidt was in the news. For a little while, when it was a novelty, the media contacted her for a quick comment when other Canadian soldiers were killed. It was not surprising the media kept in touch. She was the young, attractive widow who had spoken so eloquently at her husband's funeral, who seemed to embody a nation's grief, and shock, at the first deaths in Afghanistan.

Then she disappeared. A Google search shows news stories until 2004, a few references after that, and then nothing.

"It was a conscious decision," she says, when a reporter tracks her down. "I had been in the paper for so long, I didn't want to be there anymore. I needed my privacy."

Marley still lives in Edmonton. She has remarried and has two daughters, aged three and one. She has started working again, part-time, at the insurance company where she was working when Marc died. She has very little contact anymore with the Edmonton Garrison, although she was once a fixture at the family support centre. Most of Marc's old friends in the 3rd Battalion don't know how to contact her.

While initially surprised when a reporter phoned her unlisted number, she agreed to a short interview. In the back of her mind, she says, she knew that with the ten-year anniversary approaching she would be talking about it to someone soon. She says:

> I think about Marc every day, he's in my life every day, and I hope he's happy for me. I think he would be.
>
> I have some control again. I had very little control in the beginning. Marc died in seconds, but you know, he had a full life before that. People forget that. His death, it became what he was. What I was.
>
> … After his death I got a degree in social work. For a while I thought I would get into the field, maybe work overseas, a place like the Livno Valley. That was the idea at one time. But things change. I'm married now. I have two young daughters. The social work thing has to be put on hold for a while.
>
> … I've thought about the Afghan mission a lot, especially recently. I never thought we would be there for ten years. Marc would have been surprised too. I think he would have been proud of what we did over there, but he would have thought it was time to leave.
>
> You know, we did so much over there, but we paid such a price, parts of it were so tragic. Marc probably would have told me "that's war." I can imagine him saying that. It's a difficult question, saying whether it was worth it. Maybe it's not my place to say. I'm not a soldier.
>
> It's funny talking about this now because back then, right after it happened, I went into therapy and my counsellor told me I needed to get myself to a healthy place, that I needed to really work at that, so that ten years down the road I would have some sort of life. And here it is, ten years down the road.
>
> I think I'm in a good place. I feel that I am.

At the end of the interview Marley asked that her married name not be published.

Marc Léger's parents need no reminders that ten years have passed since the Afghan mission began. All they need is to stare out their living room window.

When Corporal Robbie Beerenfenger and Sergeant Robert Short were killed in Kabul, they were the first Canadian soldiers killed in Afghanistan since Tarnak Farm. Claire and Richard Léger debated, when they heard of the soldiers' deaths, what they should do about the Canadian flags in their front yard. The four flags that had been placed there in the spring of 2002 were still there. They had thought of removing them when the snow had come later that year, then decided against it, feeling it was not right to displace the flags. When spring came they were surprised to see the flags had fared well. The bright red had only faded a little. No ripping or tearing. So the flags stayed in their rock garden.

Now they had to decide whether to keep their makeshift memorial as a tribute to their son and his three fallen comrades, or should it become a tribute to all the Canadian soldiers killed in Afghanistan? That was the debate in the fall of 2003, whether to honour four or to honour six. Perhaps it was the simplicity of such a thing, the slight numeric extension, that ended up making the Légers decision an easy one. They went out and bought two more flags.

By the autumn of 2011 there were 159 flags in their rock garden.

Canadian flags in front of Claire and Richard Léger's home in Ottawa. There is one flag for each soldier killed in Afghanistan.

"We never intended on having so many," said Claire Léger. "But once you start, how do you stop?"

There are other reminders of their son inside their home. Portraits of him hang on several walls. Photo albums are on a coffee table. What happened at Tarnak Farm is never far removed for the Légers, who still struggle with what happened that day. Trying to make some sense of it is a pursuit that so far has produced meagre results, and got harder as the years went by, not easier. Today, thinking about the Afghan mission leaves them both bitter.

Things were not always that way. Claire Léger was a Silver Cross Mother in 2005, when the front yard of her home was still mostly grass and perennial flowers, not Canadian flags. She did her duties admirably, laid a wreath at the National War Memorial during Remembrance Day ceremonies, looked appropriately stoic for photographs as she stood next to Governor General Adrienne Clarkson, spoke to reporters afterward, about Marc, and the renewed mission in Afghanistan, and how some good might come from the death of her son by the rebuilding of that war-torn country.

Sergeant Marc Léger lifting weights while on deployment to the Livno Valley, Bosnia.

Then the Canadians were redeployed to Kandahar, and the deaths started to climb. The Canadian flags in front of her home doubled, then doubled again, until finally it seemed a mockery, her son being the first in such a long line of deaths that had accomplished, well, what exactly? That was the question that, once asked and not answered, never went away. Claire Léger began speaking out against the Afghan mission, saying it no longer made sense. By 2010, when Stephen Harper was posing for photographs with the mothers of fallen soldiers, photos taken in Ottawa where she lives, Claire Léger was no longer invited.

Richard Léger also became bitter. Not only because of his son's death, and what it had done to his wife, but for the deaths that followed. He agreed with his wife. Canadian soldiers dying in a place like Afghanistan made no sense. They should have ended the mission a long time ago; deployed the troops someplace else. Haiti, perhaps, a country in their own hemisphere, a country that needed help, and that didn't have suicide bombers, IEDs, and a hundred other ways for soldiers to die a stupid, pointless death.

Of course, life is not cause and effect, a shaving of one thing, the adding of another. He is old enough to realize that, and aware of the other arguments for deploying to Afghanistan, the other justifications for a soldier's death: international stature, treaty obligations, finishing a task. And while for some those arguments may have rung true, in his opinion it was sideways thinking, glancing logic, a convoluted explanation given by politicians and generals for something that could not be explained. Bottom line is: soldiers had died. For no good reason.

In Richard Léger's own words:

> People want to believe in the mission, because we have so much invested in it. If you even question it, some people get upset. They say it's an insult to the soldiers who died, some sort of disrespect.
>
> Well, my son was one of the first soldiers to die, and I'm here to tell you it's not disrespectful to question it. It's not a slight to the soldiers. Marc was a good soldier. Everyone over there did an incredible job, under

extremely tough circumstances. Canada has some of the best soldiers in the world.

But did we send them to the right place? That's a fair question.

In autumn of 2011 the Légers were again in the news, when Claire Léger questioned the government's decision not to immediately erect a memorial to the soldiers who had fallen in Afghanistan. While the combat mission had ended in July, and the Canadian Forces had plans to erect a permanent memorial, perhaps next to the National War Memorial in Ottawa, the plans were scuttled by the federal government, who argued the mission wouldn't truly end until 2014, when the training component had finished. The government would consider a memorial then.

To Léger, and many political pundits and military commentators, the move stank of politics, a tactic by the government to keep the deaths in Afghanistan out of the news. More than one person commented on the fact there had been no ceremony in Canada to mark the end of the combat mission. While the beginning, Operation Apollo, had seen prime ministers waving goodbye to ships, and defence ministers addressing troops at the Edmonton Garrison — the media duly alerted to the photo opportunities — the ending had nothing. It just petered away.

Pat McGrath, Ottawa Citizen

Silver Cross Mother Claire Léger with her husband, Richard, at Remembrance Day ceremonies in Ottawa, 2005.

* * *

In 2011 Lloyd Smith took down the memorial to his son. He had sold the farm in Tatamagouche and was moving to an apartment in Dartmouth.

Selling the farm was tough, but with just he and his wife living there, it was too much work maintaining a century-old farm, close enough to the Northumberland Straits to be stung by salt air and strong winds most days of the year. He is a man accustomed to hard work, thought of keeping the farm even though the maintenance filled his days, but in the end decided he needed the break. So did his wife.

It was tough taking down the cairns. As tough as selling the farm. In nine years he had added to them, modified them, built around them, created something people in Tatamagouche brought out-of-town visitors to see, the same way visitors were brought to fisherman's wharfs and light-houses. He had finished the white picket fence and the flower beds. Had put up wooden plaques to Marc Léger, Ainsworth Dyer, and Ricky Green, put them on the base of the flagpoles where the Canadian flag, Princess Patricia's flag, and Alpha Company's flag flew. For Nathan he had built a stone marker, and imbedded a metal plaque. Nathan had been his son. He figured he should be allowed the distinction, although he worried from time to time whether he was being disrespectful to the other soldiers.

Charlotte tended the gardens, and that probably helped bring people out to see the cairns. The flowers were beautiful, bloomed from early spring to late fall, having been chosen carefully. Charlotte tended to the beds each day while Lloyd puttered around the farm, doing odd jobs. The beds ran from flag pole to flag pole, set out as a triangle with the stone marker to Nathan in front. Although he had not planned it, a company that sold aerial photos came to his door one day, after having flown over the farm taking pictures, now wanting to sell them, and from the sky it looked like a cross had been erected next to the farm.

He had thought about having some sort of ceremony when he took the flags down for the last time, but in the end he lowered them with only Charlotte standing beside him. Then they put them in a box for the move to Dartmouth.

By then he was back at work. That had been another reason to sell the farm. He had retired from Algoma Tankers in 2004, tried the retired life for a few years, tinkering in his workshop, tending to a small vegetable garden, having little interest in travel or changing his life anymore than it had already been changed. When five years passed and Algoma contacted him to ask if he would be interested in returning to sea, well, he told his wife it was a good offer, an unexpected offer, and he should accept it, although he had secretly been glad they'd phoned.

"It's pretty easy work," he would say, when a reporter contacted him in the autumn of 2011. "I'm not at sea for long stretches the way I was in the past. I guess they know I'm in my sixties now. I had to do some studying, to get my papers up to date, but it's nice being back."

He goes on to say he received a wedding invitation in the mail recently from Jodi Carter, Nathan's fiancée, who had kept in touch, visiting them every time she returned home to Nova Scotia. When Nathan had died she was studying at the University of Alberta to become a doctor, wanted to become a brain surgeon of all things, and she had done it. She was moving to Minnesota after the wedding, where she had been offered a job at the Mayo Clinic. Jodi was a good girl, and had always treated them well. He knew for some of the other families things had not gone as well. No accounting for sorrow, he supposed. They say time heals all things, but that's not true. Time can make a right mess out of things too.

Before the reporter hangs up he asks about the Afghan mission. Yes, Lloyd has given it plenty of thought. Ten years is a long time. And the soldiers that fell, you would be surprised how many came from the Maritimes. Afghanistan will be a part of many lives in the Maritimes for a long time.

"I'm proud of what Nathan did," he tells the reporter. "I'm proud he served his country. It was a worthwhile mission and I'm glad we tried to help the people in Afghanistan. Lord knows they needed our help."

Doreen Young was arrested in 2004, when the RCMP were called to the house she and her husband bought with the money from Ricky's insurance payout. It was a domestic dispute and the cops charged both of them, although neither agreed to testify so the charges were later dropped.

Young's marriage ended shortly afterward. She moved back to the trailer where she had raised her only child, bitter most days that the lawyers worked it out so her husband got the house, still not comprehending exactly how that went down. The truth is that things have not gone well since Ricky died. She's not sure if that was the tipping point, but before April 17, 2002, she had a son, a husband, a life that finally seemed to be turning a corner, and very quickly she had none of that. Maybe there's no connection. Maybe it's just coincidence. How do you ever know about these things?

She tried to sue the United States government for wrongful death after Ricky died, but that didn't turn out well either. If you're a cannery worker from Hubbards, Nova Scotia, the United States government is one tough foe, and the suit didn't last long. Something to do with jurisdiction, she didn't follow it all. Just ended up wasting her time, and annoying a lot of people around Hubbards, who said she was looking for blood money. Ricky's fiancé, Miranda, became her most vocal critic. She hears Miranda is married now. It's been a long time since they talked, and running into her on the street would be unpleasant.

The Department of National Defence flew her to Afghanistan one year, so she could see where Ricky died. They did that for a lot of families if they asked, which she did. They would give you an escort officer, like she had that first year, and they would fly you to Afghanistan. She had expected to be taken right to Tarnak Farm, but when she got there she

Private Richard Green, in Afghanistan.

was told it was too dangerous. Some soldiers had died the week before, so she had to settle for walking to the top of an observation tower, where a soldier gave her a pair of binoculars, pointed her in the right direction, where she could see some old stone walls, a bunch of what looked like irrigation ditches, and he said: "Right there, you're looking at it."

On her way down from the observation tower, while walking on the wooden steps, her steps got lighter and lighter, like some sort of weight was falling away. It was probably as close to a religious experience as she had ever come, if that was the right way to describe it.

She started using her maiden name a few years ago. Paid to have her ex-husband's name taken off Ricky's tombstone. Money she really didn't have, because she's back doing janitorial work, but it was important that it be done. Maybe, if you were outside looking in, you could say her life is tough. About as tough as it's ever been, she will tell a reporter when he contacts her, but she's learned a few lessons over the years. You know what they say about whatever doesn't kill you? Don't spend any time feeling sorry for her.

She sends a few emails to the reporter, when he has some questions. As with all her emails, they end with a postscript, "Oh death, where is thy sting! It has none. But life has."

Agatha Dyer says at least once a week she has a dream about Ainsworth. A good dream is Ainsworth walking through her door — it seems to be Christmas — and her son lifts her off her feet and twirls her around, the photos in her apartment swirling around her like she's on a merry-go-round: Ainsworth as a young boy, a waterfall in Jamaica, her daughter in her nurse's whites. Ainsworth whispers in her ear, "What have you made for me Mom? I'm hungry." A bad dream has nothing at all. It's black. Nothing but the sound of her boy moaning somewhere while Agatha tries to find him.

She lives in the same Montreal apartment that Ainsworth used to visit, the place where he told her once he was getting married, bringing his fiancée with him, Jocelyn, such a beautiful girl. Agatha had immediately thought of grandchildren, perhaps relocating to Edmonton. They would need the help. Now Jocelyn does not even speak to her. She said it was too much, the fighting between Agatha and Ainsworth's dad. Said she needed to move on.

Many people told Agatha to do the same thing, but Paul getting all the insurance money and not sharing it with anyone was not right. Paul got to buy a condominium, get out of social housing, while she had no such change in life. She was left with nothing but photos and bad dreams. Although some dreams are good, she had to admit that, Ainsworth coming home, or standing near cool pools of water in Jamaica, a dream so vivid and detailed she had to remind herself from time to time that Ainsworth had been born in Montreal and there was no true memory of such a thing.

Paul Dyer always said he would have traded his condominium in a heartbeat if it would bring back his only son, and those who knew him never doubted it. The loss of his "baby" was never something he could accept. He had loved that boy, taken comfort from him, from the man he became, gave him a belief in a system of cause and effect that governed the natural world, despite all the conflicting evidence. His beautiful reward. That had been Ainsworth Dyer.

When Ainsworth died, Paul Dyer lost that faith. Religion was a poor substitute after that. Something hollow and contrived. The elders at his church tried to help, but nothing could stop him from sinking deeper and deeper into despair, the words of the Good Book failing to rouse his spirits, the stories and parables no longer resonating, no longer finding a place in his heart, just words he now doubted, or scorned.

Paul Dyer died in 2004. He passed away in the condominium purchased with his son's insurance money. It was several days before anyone found his body.

EPILOGUE

The early days of November 2011 were unseasonably warm in the nation's capital. The temperature was often in double digits and there were vegetables left growing in backyard gardens, boats still out on the Rideau River. Many hardwood trees had leaves on their lower branches, an odd sight that no one could recall seeing before. On Remembrance Day I awoke early and phoned Pat Stogran. "The main entrance of the War Museum," he repeated, after we had spoken for a few minutes. "I'll see you at 10:30."

I made a pot of coffee and started reading the day's newspapers. Stories about wars, past and present, Canadian soldiers giving opinions on the Afghan mission, Second World War veterans talking about Ortona, Korean Veterans talking about Kapyong. While I read, a rain-squall blew through and by the time I started driving to the War Museum the streets were slick, culverts jammed with brown, sodden leaves that had finally fallen.

Along the way I thought of conversations I had had recently with soldiers. It was the final days of writing this book and I was double-checking facts, probing for one last anecdote, thanking people for their help. Earlier in the week I had spoken to Jason Mann, a former jumper with A Company, a soldier who had spent the morning of April 18th, 2002, picking up body parts at Tarnak Farm.

After receiving my email, he phoned from Fort St. John, British Columbia. He was using a company phone, which he quickly said was decent of his employer, giving him an office, lending him a phone, leaving him alone to make the call, all of four days into his new job. He is a trucker now, working the oil rigs around Fort St. John, about nineteen hours north of Vancouver, near the Yukon border.

He told me he'd had a lot of jobs in the seven years since he was mustered out of the army. Some were good, some were bad, not a lot of difference, really, between the good and the bad. He didn't have much of a complaint about any of them. He just couldn't keep them. He said:

I couldn't hold a job to save my live. I'd work for a couple of months, a couple of weeks. Some jobs I had just for a day or two, and then I'd quit. It was the oddest thing because I'd always be pumped about starting a new job, looking forward to it, went through all the work of getting it, you'd think that would mean something. But I'd always up and quit.

I've wondered why a person would do a thing like that. It's not that I mind working. So, am I crazy? Am I the world's biggest loser? You know what I came up with? What I think was happening? It was the army — life in the army — because in the army you spend so much time wanting to go home, wanting to come back from Bosnia, or Afghanistan, but you never could. You were in the army right?

But in the civy world, you can do that. And sure as shit, whatever job I had, there would come a day when I was working away and suddenly I would start missing my wife, missing my son, I would have this near physical desire to see them. So I'd quit and go home.

He'd been in the Canadian Forces just shy of ten years, a lot of that time as a jumper, which is how he ended up at the Edmonton Garrison, attached to the 3rd Battalion. He told me about his last jump: it was at Wainwright, Alberta, a night jump, the plane taxi-cabbing for what seemed like hours, just circling over the jump zone waiting for the winds to die, and when the company finally jumped, well, as soon as he was out the door he could tell the winds were too strong. Maybe someone got impatient. Maybe the winds picked back up. He couldn't be sure. He never spent that much time thinking about it, either. He was about to get fucked up. So was every other jumper. Simple story.

His parachute was blown in about halfway through the jump. The wind just pushed it in, like crushing an eggshell, and he fell through the darkness, not a lot of stars out, just free-falling through some black chasm, waiting to hit, wondering, for just a second, how a thing like that was going to feel. He stood up when he landed, which is another strange thing, because medically speaking he shouldn't have been able to do that, but adrenaline kicks in when you're jumping, it's like some crazy, zipped-up drug, so he stood up and tried to walk, even took a step or two before he fell and then he just lay there in the field, hearing the moans of other jumpers lying in the darkness around him.

Another jumper found him and put a light beside him, so the medics knew to check him out. When a medic came he asked him what was wrong and Mann told him.

"I can't walk. My knees are all fucked. My back feels fucked."

"We'll come back for you," said the medic.

And he lay there wondering if he had spoken in his own head, not been able to make the words audible, because he had just told the medic he thought his back was broken, and how the hell could a guy move on after hearing that? Wasn't till the next day he learned the jumper next to him had a broken neck.

He never jumped after that. Started driving a truck. It was the one skill the army taught him that turned out to be useful. It got him the job in Fort St. John, and a lot of other jobs too. The town was booming, and it looked all right. Flat country, which you wouldn't expect in northern British Columbia, but it's in the Peace River Valley, about two hours east of the Rockies. The town motto is "The Energetic City," which he doesn't understand, but like he said, he'd only been there four days.

Going from jumper to truck driver was a tough transition. But he wanted to stay in the army, loved the job right up to the day he was given a medical discharge and told to leave. He still missed it. And that was another thing he wondered about, same way he wondered why he couldn't hang onto a job. He even tried to re-enlist once, and explain that one. Why would a sane man go back to the people who kicked him out three months before he was eligible for a ten-year pension? Not that the pension would have been much, but it would have been something, right? Something more than what he got, which was a medical discharge for having post traumatic stress disorder, and his hearing all fucked up, and his back never quite right again — a lot of things — although it was mostly PTSD.

So why would he miss a thing like that? After seven years of knockabout jobs he thinks he has the answer. It was the camaraderie. The friendship.

It was like a brotherhood, being in the army. Sure, that's a cliché, damn straight it is, but that doesn't make it any less true. No matter how good a day he's having right now, he would trade it in for a good day from the past.

We talked for more than two hours, until he finally said he had to hang up. He'd told his boss he'd only be on the phone for a couple hours, and four days into a new job he should probably do what he says. He can phone back, though. Give him a couple of days.

"I'm guessing you want to talk about the friendly fire thing," he says.

"I do."

"I figured you would. Strange to think it's been nearly ten years. I remember it like it was yesterday. What the weather was like, how things smelt. Like I just woke up in Kandahar."

"I want to talk about other things, too."

"Like what?"

"Everything. You guys were the first ones over there. I want to talk about deploying, OP Harpoon. I want to know what thoughts were going through your head when you first got there."

"To Afghanistan?"

"That's right."

He didn't answer right away. Over the phone came the sound of a door opening, a muffled voice, chairs scrapping, then he was back. "I got to phone you back, but shit, I can tell you right now what I was thinking when I got to Kandahar: I was thinking: 'Jason, this is going to be the longest, most fucked-up thing you've ever done.'"

I wondered if that were true. Was Afghanistan the longest, most fucked up thing the Canadian military had ever done? It was a decade-long military operation that drained the Canadian treasury of anywhere from twelve to eighteen billion dollars, cost the lives of 159 men and women — 189 if you included suicides, accidents, and non-military personnel — and at the end of the day had accomplished — what? Not even the most giddy optimist, or the most craven apologist, thought the odds of Canada having affected lasting change in Afghanistan were anything better than maybe yes, maybe no. That was what we had earned after all our toil and sacrifice. A coin toss.

I knew a lot of soldiers agreed with Mann. I had spoken to them. And yet there were others, some of the best soldiers in the Canadian Forces, who didn't. Among them was Steve Borland, a soldier with a bronze star on his parade uniform, who had kept the 3rd Battalion running a lot of days in Afghanistan, yet he had landed in a rehab clinic in Nanaimo, suffering from PTSD, alcoholism, drug addiction. If there was a man I was expecting to dump all over Afghanistan, he was it.

But he didn't. Earlier that autumn I had visited Borland's home at Canadian Forces Base Kingston, where he had recently been transferred from the Edmonton Garrison. His home is on a bluff with a fine view of the Kingston Harbour, the Cataraqui River, and the copper roof of a Martello Tower build by Lieutenant-Colonel John By in 1830.

Under the branches of a black maple, Borland sat in a lawn chair and said his life is good now. At the age of forty-eight he has his first child. A boy by the name of Rowan, with thin red hair and brown eyes the hue of a well-burnished bar. He'll marry Rowan's mother as soon as his divorce is final.

To this day he's hard pressed to explain why he began drinking after his second tour of Afghanistan. He doesn't think it was military service that made him drink, even if there were things that happened on his second tour in Afghanistan that bother him to this day.

He was close to Glyn Berry, the Canadian diplomat killed in January 2006 when a suicide bomber rammed his Jeep. Two other civilians were killed and ten people were wounded that day, including Master-Corporal Paul Franklin, who lost both legs. Berry is the only person from Foreign Affairs to die in theatre in Afghanistan.

Borland remembered:

> He volunteered to go there. He was an old man. Well, not that old, but well into his fifties. That's a young man's game, being in theatre. Glyn didn't have to be there. He shouldn't have been there.
>
> After he died, it was never the same for the provincial reconstruction teams. The humanitarian work, the going out to the villages and building wells, doing

medical checks, it all came to a halt. It was years before it got going again.

Our civilian partners, CIDA, Foreign Affairs, after Glyn died they all reined things in. It was like they suddenly realized Afghanistan was a dangerous place. Well, you know what? It *was* a fuckin' dangerous place.

Borland wishes the reconstruction work had continued. He thinks the Afghan mission would have been quite different if it had. He says after Berry's death the mission became a chicken-and-egg debate. Do you engage in reconstruction, in the hope that it will make the country more secure? Or do you seek out the enemy, to make the area more secure for reconstruction? Canada opted for seeking out the enemy, and most of the Canadian soldiers killed in Afghanistan died after that decision was made.

"We lost a lot of corporate memory when we abandoned the reconstruction efforts in 2006," said Borland. "It was years before we were back to the same level."

Lieutenant-Colonel Steven Borland outside his home in Kingston.

As we talked, a late-model Sebring pulled into his driveway. The driver's door swung open and a statuesque woman with raven-coloured hair stepped out and gave a shy wave. She walked to the back passenger door, leaned in, then pulled herself back out while a boy scampered after her. Rowan. He made an uneven run toward the tree, Borland already starting to stand, shoving a package of cigarettes into a pocket of his jeans, spreading his arms.

"I think we're back on track now. I think it's the right mission," he said. "Training the Afghan army, the Afghan police. Every soldier I know supports that mission."

The young boy is swept into the air. In the background there is deep water and a ferry making its way to Wolfe Island.

The oldest soldier I ever met was Paul Métivier. I met him at Cabaret-Rouge Cemetery, in Northern France, just down the road from Vimy Ridge, when he was one hundred years old.

Cabaret Rouge Cemetery is where Canada's Unknown Soldier once lay, and Métivier was in France as part of a Canadian delegation bringing his body home. It was the spring of 2000, and I remember thinking, when I met him in a hotel room in Arras, getting dressed for dinner, putting on his blue Legionnaire's jacket, that he didn't look that bad for a century-old man.

Métivier had fought at Vimy Ridge. Since the soldier being exhumed and brought back to Canada had been laid to rest in a grave not far from Vimy, it was assumed he also had fought there. Métivier had been invited to France as a living link to the Unknown Soldier, an almost ceremonial gesture on the part of Veteran's Affairs, although he was the only one in the delegation who, when the body was exhumed, could explain to the French coroner why the soldier had been buried still wearing his gas mask.

"He would have been rolled into a blanket when they found him," Métivier explained to the doctor. "Nothing was ever removed. Roll into a blanket, drag away, clear the path. Those were the orders."

And thus the coroner had his answer, not only for the gas mask, but also for the boots on the soldier's feet.

Métivier was sixteen when he enlisted for the First World War at a recruiting office in Montreal, lying about his age and being shipped to England as part of the Canadian Expeditionary Force. He was at Vimy the following year. He told me once what he remembered best about Vimy was the mud. He was surprised when he returned eighty-three years later and discovered a verdant green hill surrounded by pastures. The mud surrounding Vimy Ridge in 1917 was deep enough to swallow a mule. That was his job — escorting a mule back and forth to the artillery lines, eight shells per mule, ironic since he had wanted to join the cavalry, so he could ride horses and fight the enemy. Instead he got a mule.

In the late spring of 1918 his commanding officers finally learned his true age, and Métivier was shipped back to England. He arrived in Montreal two weeks before Armistice was declared. He had a good life after that. Married, had five children, learned a trade — photo engraver at the then Department of the Interior, where he worked until he retired in 1965.

Back in Ottawa, where we both lived, I spoke to him often. Métivier was an active man — walked every day to pick up a newspaper, did his shopping at an outdoor market. When he moved into a seniors' home at the age of 101, he complained to me that there was no gym. Thought that might merit a story. He had strong opinions on what he read in the newspapers, the folly still unfolding around him, and from time to time would comment on my work, telling me occasionally that I had come close to the truth with a certain column, but just missed the mark.

I would often see him at the Remembrance Day ceremony in downtown Ottawa. In 2002 I bumped into him in front of the National War Memorial, both of us remarking on the large crowd that had assembled that year, and the spontaneous act we'd witnessed after the ceremony, when people started removing their poppies and placing them on the tomb of the Unknown Soldier.

"Look at this," said Métivier, staring at the blanket of poppies covering the tomb. "I hope there is a picture of this in your newspaper tomorrow."

"I bet there will be."

"Yes, a good front-page photo. It would be wrong if you didn't do that."

We talked after that about the large crowd, wondering what had brought them out, what had made them stay after the final wreath was placed, to lay poppies on the tomb. The weather often seemed to discourage large crowds for this ceremony — in recent years it had snowed, rained, hailed, been bitterly cold; there often seemed to be metaphysical gremlins at work in Ottawa on Remembrance Day, the weather as somber as the notes of the Last Post — but that had not happened this year.

"It's the deaths in Afghanistan," I remember saying. "People have come to honour the four soldiers." Métivier said I was right, but felt there was something else at work. Again, I was close, but had missed the mark. I had to stop doing that.

"People are remembering what it means to be a soldier," he said. "That's why they have come."

Paul Métivier died two years later, three days before Christmas. He was 104. He was one of the last half-dozen First World War veterans still living in Canada.

I find Pat Stogran talking to a naval officer outside the War Museum boutique, the officer knows him from when they worked together in Kingston. The museum is now crowded, people coming up to talk to Stogran fairly regularly, people he used to work with, people who recognize him from the many times he was on television or in the newspaper as Veterans Ombudsman. A few thank him for what he tried to do for Afghan veterans.

"Don't know if I did all that much," he says to me, when the crowd around him disperses. "They threw my ass out."

We walk around the boutique for a few moments, examining the displays of military books, regimental ties, children's compasses and survival kits. We pause in front of a rack of fatigue-green hoodies, a peace sign emblazoned on the front.

"I like those," says Stogran, pointing to the hoodies. "I may get one. I'm becoming a bit of a peacenik these days."

It is a strange comment to hear from this man who once cobbled together a worldview from slogans taught at martial arts classes and lines from *The Devil's Brigade*. As I stand there, I realize there is probably no one I have interviewed who changed more because of the Afghan mission than Pat Stogran. He went into the conflict with a bravado that actually scared the generals sitting at their desks back in Ottawa, was told more than once to tone down the language, stop wearing the maroon beret, don't actually come right out and say it was disappointing not to find any al Qaeda fighters to kill while humping around the Whale. Now he's standing in a store, saying he might buy a peace hoodie.

He was diagnosed with PTSD after he returned from Afghanistan — whether because of Kandahar, or Goražde, he can't say, and it probably doesn't make much of a difference. It happened. You deal with it.

Today he is trying to get a consulting business off the ground. Surprised by how much it costs to incorporate a company in Canada. Wishing he could get more invitations to speak at universities and colleges, the way it was when he was Veterans Ombudsman.

At 10:45 we are escorted into Memorial Hall. I have invited Stogran to the War Museum to see something that is one of the marvels of modern architecture, even though it is a stolen idea that goes back millennia. Back to Chichen Itza in Mexico, the Chaco Canyon in New Mexico.

Memorial Hall is a small, stone-walled room in the National War Museum with a gun-slit-shaped window on its back wall, and nothing on the front wall but the headstone of the Unknown Soldier. The tombstone was taken from Cabaret-Rouge Cemetery on the same day the Unknown Soldier's body was exhumed. It has a faded cross and a short inscription that reads: "A soldier of the great war, a Canadian regiment, known unto God."

About three-dozen people stand in Memorial Hall with us, shuffling their feet, looking at their watches. Among them are several veterans of the Second World War. I had spoken to each of them on the way into the room, and knew the youngest was eighty-eight. Canada loses five hundred Second World War veterans every week. There are now an estimated 125,000 left, slightly more than one-tenth the number that once served. I look around, wondering if the next Paul Métivier could be among us.

While I am doing that, a slender band of light enters Memorial Hall. It lands on the front wall, to the left of the tombstone. As we watch it widens, brightens, and inches closer to the tombstone. Then, as we hear a

PA announcement say we have come to the eleventh hour, of the eleventh day, of the eleventh month, the room fills with light.

It is as though a switch has been turned on, it is so sudden. The sun refracts off the white marble of the tombstone, obscuring the cross and the insignia, becomes a bright, diffused orb hovering above the ground. It is left to each of us to decide what the headstone most resembles at that moment — the beam of a lighthouse; a cookfire in the bush, suddenly spied through the trees; the rear muzzle flash of an 84-mm Carl Gustav recoilless rifle on a pitch-black night.

Then, just as suddenly, the sun is gone. The clouds have obviously moved outside. When a minute passes, and the sun doesn't return, the room getting steadily darker, we begin to leave. Several people stop to place a poppy on the lip of the tombstone. Some of the veterans wipe away tears, furtive taps on their cheeks that they try to hide.

We drive to Mello's, what is normally a short drive taking nearly an hour. Many of the streets in downtown Ottawa are closed, throngs of people making their way back from the ceremony in front of the National War

Pat Stogran at Mello's Diner in Ottawa.

Memorial. The crowds have become bigger each year since the Afghan Mission started. When we get to the diner a waitress who doesn't want to go home in the afternoons is waiting for us. We have a long lunch. Watch the rain come.

More than once I am tempted to ask the commander of the first Canadian soldiers into Afghanistan what he was thinking, when the sun refracted off the headstone of the Unknown Soldier, but never get around to it. Sometimes you don't need an answer. Or a conclusion. It is enough to have been there.

Of Related Interest

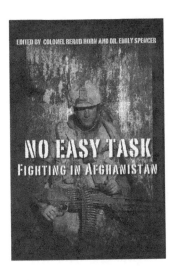

No Easy Task
Fighting in Afghanistan
Edited by Colonel Bernd Horn and Dr. Emily Spencer
978-1-459701625
$35.00

Afghanistan has long been considered the graveyard of empires. Throughout their history, Afghans have endured the ravages of foreign invaders, from marauding hordes and imperial armies to global super-powers, while demonstrating a fierce independence and strong resistance to outside occupiers. Those who have ventured into Afghanistan with notions of controlling its people have soon discovered that fighting in that rugged, hostile land is no easy task. Afghans have proven to be tenacious and unrelenting foes.

No Easy Task examines this legacy of conflict, particularly from a Canadian perspective. What emerges is the difficulty faced by foreign forces attempting to impose their will over Afghans who, for their part, have consistently adapted tactics and strategies to stymie and defeat those they perceive as invaders and interlopers. It is within this complexity and challenge that the difficult counter-insurgency must be fought.

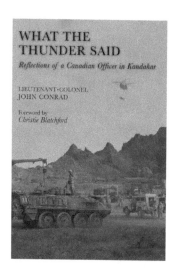

What the Thunder Said
Reflections of a Canadian Officer in Kandahar
Lieutenant-Colonel John Conrad
978-1-554884087
$29.95

By every principle of war, every shred of military logic, logistics support to Canada's Task Force Orion in Afghanistan should have collapsed in July 2006. There are few countries that offer a greater challenge to logistics than Afghanistan, and yet Canadian soldiers lived through an enormous test on this deadly international stage — a monumental accomplishment. Canadian combat operations were widespread across southern Afghanistan in 2006, and logistics soldiers worked in quiet desperation to keep the battle group moving. Only now is it appreciated how precarious the logistics operations of Task Force Orion in Kandahar really were.

What the Thunder Said is an honest, raw recollection of incidents and impressions of Canadian warfighting from a logistics perspective. It offers solid insight into the history of military logistics in Canada and explores in some detail the dramatic erosion of a once-proud corner of the army from the perspective of a battalion commander.

Available at your favourite bookseller.

DUNDURN
www.dundurn.com

What did you think of this book?
Visit *www.dundurn.com* for reviews, videos, updates, and more!